Revenge of the Women's Studies Professor

Bonnie J. Morris

**Indiana
University
Press**
Bloomington and
Indianapolis

This book is a publication of

Indiana University Press
601 North Morton Street
Bloomington, IN 47404-3797 USA

http://iupress.indiana.edu

Telephone orders	800-842-6796
Fax orders	812-855-7931
Orders by e-mail	iuporder@indiana.edu

© 2009 by Bonnie J. Morris
All rights reserved

The paper used in this publication meets the minimum
requirements of American National Standard for Information
Sciences—Permanence of Paper for Printed Library Materials,
ANSI Z39.48-1984.

Manufactured in the United States of America

Library of Congress Cataloging-in-Publication Data

Morris, Bonnie J., [date]
 Revenge of the women's studies professor / Bonnie J. Morris.
  p. cm.
 Includes bibliographical references and index.
 ISBN 978-0-253-35295-8 (cl) — ISBN 978-0-253-22062-2
(pbk) 1. Women's studies—United States. 2. Feminism and
higher education—United States. I. Title.
 HQ1181.U5M67 2009
 305.40973—dc22
                                        2008030346

 2 3 4 5   14 13 12 11 10

To every student who has dared to take a
women's studies class

and

with love to the friends I made during
graduate school at Binghamton,
women who taught me to study, write,
love, and act in equal measure

What I really lacked was simply enough distance
from my experience to know how to use it.

—Jane Rule

We have achieved identity, but we are far, far
from achieving equality.

—Gloria Steinem

Contents

Acknowledgments

Many, many people have helped me to become a professor cheerfully stand-ing alone on a stage talking about women's studies. I begin with loving thanks to my teachers at Carolina Friends School, notably Don and Darlene Wells, who encouraged me to enroll in my first women's studies class, and Henry Walker, writing mentor to the CFS generations. For years of dramatic training and performance opportunities, I'm grateful to Allied Arts of the Durham Theatre Guild; Adventure Theatre in Glen Echo, Maryland; and the Depart-ment of Performing Arts at American University in Washington, D.C. For introduction to feminist production values, I honor my friends at Herizon in Binghamton, plus the many producers, techies, and artists of the Michigan Women's Music Festival, the National Women's Music Festival, the Gulf Coast Women's Festival, the Northeast Women's Music Retreat, Campfest, and the East Coast Lesbian Festival. Particular honor to the late Brenda Henson of Camp Sister Spirit, in loving memory. For the opportunity to meet Lily Tom-lin, I thank Adele Brown and Faith Rogow. Kind hosts of my performances outside the United States include Prue Hyman and Carolyn Michelle in New Zealand; Irma Erlingsdottir in Reykjavik, Iceland; Tal Jarus in Tel Aviv, Israel; the Women's Education, Research and Resource Center at University College, Dublin, Ireland; and Sheena Howard at Queen's College in Kingston, Ontario, Canada. For wonderful and fulfilling teaching appointments which afforded much writing and performance time, I thank Constance Buchanan at Harvard Divinity School and Jeanne Henry at Northern Kentucky University. And for securing my ongoing adjunct professorships in Washington, D.C., including the opportunity to teach Athletics and Gender, I'm enormously beholden to Diane Bell, Barbara Miller, and Dan Moshenberg at George Washington Uni-versity, and to Leslie Byers, Pamela Fox, Sue Thomas, and Suzanna Walters at Georgetown.

An earlier, abbreviated version of "Educating President Clinton" appeared in *That Takes Ovaries!*, edited by Rivka Solomon; Three Rivers Press, 2002. An excerpt in "Fear of the Word *Woman*" was published as "The Scholar's Gro-ceries," edited by Fran Day, in *Sinister Wisdom* 67 (Summer 2006); and an excerpt in "You're Getting a Ph.D. in *What*?" was published as "When I Was a Teenage ERA Activist," in *NWSA Journal* 14, no. 2 (Summer 2002).

I have been fortunate to complete this manuscript while enjoying the love and encouragement of Liz Casey; my parents, Myra and Roger; the spoken-word community of Mothertongue in Washington, D.C.; and the worker community of the Michigan Women's Music Festival. One could not ask for finer companions and allies.

Finally, I am delighted to have the support of Indiana University Press. Indiana University in Bloomington, the site of the National Women's Music Festival in June 1993, is where I first performed *Revenge*.

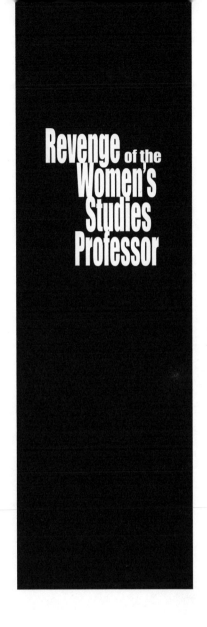

Revenge of the
Women's
Studies
Professor

Introduction
So, What Do You Do for a Living?

What I do makes people angry.

No, I'm not a terrorist. Far from it! I'm not a tax collector, or a scam artist, or a child abuser. I don't prey on the elderly or mistreat kittens. What is it about my line of work that upsets total strangers?

I'm a women's studies professor.

I teach basic women's history: the who, what, when, where, why, and how of our foremothers, black and white, rich and poor. My classes invite students to learn from the past. How did women live in the nineteenth century? In the ancient world? Which laws, or kings, or queens, determined their rights? What beliefs guided their hopes and fears, or their religious rites? Whether farmwives or artists, healers or innkeepers, servants or slaves, how did women survive the daily demands of work and family life, particularly if they had no political voice? And once women began to organize and speak out, how did they win the right to vote, the right to attend college, the right to play sports?

I love what I do; and, based on my student evaluations from the past twenty-five years, I'm good at what I do. But even now, in 2009, most college students never expose themselves to women's history. They're afraid that enrolling in a class will damage their reputation. They know that if they tell their friends they're even thinking about taking my course, if their parents see it listed on a transcript or tuition bill, or if their boyfriend hears about it, they'll be treated to a hailstorm of criticism and harassment—not unlike what I en-

OPPOSITE PAGE: First performance of *Revenge,* National Women's Music Festival, Indiana University, 1993. PHOTO BY TONI ARMSTRONG JR.

dured myself, twenty-five years ago. The backlash has existed almost as long as the frontlash, ever since the first women's studies courses became standard at American colleges and universities in the early 1970s.

"Women's studies! Are you becoming a *feminazi*?" a bystander laughed at one of my new students during the first week of classes. Thanks to radio critic Rush Limbaugh, who coined this term in the early 1990s, *feminazi* is one common form of name-calling experienced by women's studies students and faculty. Since I am Jewish, being accused of teaching Nazi values is grossly offensive—and also easy to disprove; read my syllabi and see what really goes on in a women's history class. But such name-calling flourishes, even here at George Washington University, where students hail from enlightened, well-educated families. Moreover, because Limbaugh's pet phrase quickly became part of mainstream slang, students who grew up hearing it may not be aware of how mean-spirited it is; a young woman popped into my office hours last semester to confide: "I just love your class. You're different from what I expected—you're not, like, a Nazi or anything!" On another occasion, a freshman cheerfully sent me this note: "I thought I'd be the only guy in the class, surrounded by a roomful of girls who are all male-bashers like the psycho-feminist bitch teaching the class. Signing up was my last resort. But I'm surprised. I like it so far." I can't imagine any other academic discipline where students feel entitled, during the first week of class, to compliment the professor for not being a psycho-feminist Nazi bitch.

"Women's studies? Oh. I didn't know you were one of *them*." This is another common remark aimed at my students, reminding them that they've crossed an invisible boundary. A scholarly interest in the accomplishments of one's foremothers equals extremism: If you care about women, you must hate men. And if you want to read about women, you must want to sample them sexually, too. A student who takes even one course in women's history thus becomes *gay*. This cascade of stereotypes would be funny if it didn't keep so many bright minds closed to important subject matter: the history of half the world.

In every era, women have sacrificed goals and desires in order to maintain a good reputation. This is just a modern version: avoiding women's studies so you won't gain a reputation as a *lezbo*. Interestingly, parents, peers, and girlfriends rarely warn young men that reading books about men's history will make them gay. Men's history is required for all students, male and female. An interest in male leadership and accomplishment is nurtured in our schoolwork from kindergarten through law school, so it's *normal* to examine the record of man.

"Women's studies! What are you going to do with *that*?" This approach suggests that courses in women's history are useless, professionally; one should only take courses in subjects that guarantee high-paying jobs after graduation. But if we follow that rule, we'll soon eliminate every one of the traditional liberal arts majors, including English, religion, philosophy, art history, dance, drama, Latin, Greek, and so on.

And, speaking of income, do any students ever begin earning big money right after graduation? Yes: the male basketball players. I've seen several student-athletes from my classes drafted, at age 21 or 22, into pro positions where they're earning far more than I ever will. If income and media visibility are guiding goals for career choices, universities will need to drop humanities requirements and steer all students into pro sports careers. I should have perfected my jump shot.

Actually, the snappy answer to "What can you do with a women's studies degree?" is *law school.* A background on women's legal status in world civilizations, from pre-biblical Babylonia to contemporary Iran and Afghanistan, is excellent preparation for a career in law or diplomacy, both of which are respectably salaried professions. Listening to and learning from women is desirable background for anyone working in international development, HIV/AIDS education, counseling, psychology, workplace management—jobs for the twenty-first century, certainly. But at most campuses, women's history is an elective, never a requirement, and so it's not seen as a serious pre-law concentration. Instead, many students assume that a class about women will be an easy A, and take it as the filler in an otherwise tough schedule. They are startled and hurt when they get a C– on that first paper and realize they are going to have to produce some real academic work.

All women's studies professors battle the stereotypes equating feminism with politically correct sexual chauvinism. Yet peek inside the classroom and most of us are teaching the basic principles of good old American democracy: how women helped in the American Revolution, helped in the Civil War, helped in World War I, and, having sacrificed their sons throughout 140 years of patriotic motherhood, were finally recognized as being worthy of the right to vote.

I wanted to talk back to the stereotypes, to make women's studies less scary, to get a conversation going about backlash. And so I wrote a one-woman play.

So here's the short version of the book you're about to read. Since 1993, I've been traveling around the world with a one-woman show called *Revenge of the Women's Studies Professor,* inviting college audiences and women's communities to talk honestly about the backlash against women's studies. I wrote the play just as the internet and e-mail were beginning to occupy more of students' time than reading, when I believed that more people would show up for an entertainment than search for my latest article in some obscure academic journal. I was right: Audiences love the show, and I'm still touring with the play fifteen years later, on top of teaching, writing, presenting papers at international conferences, and making the occasional TV or film appearance. (Women's studies *can* be a glamorous life!)

How did I come up with the idea? I knew that one person on a stage telling her story can deliver a walloping message. In 1992, Americans had yet to see Margaret Cho in *I'm the One That I Want,* or Eve Ensler's brilliant *Vagina Monologues.* Those actresses would capture our consciences soon enough. One actress, Anna Deveare Smith, was presenting phenomenal political theatre, playing multiple roles, compelling audiences to examine the racial tension behind contemporary riots in Crown Heights and Los Angeles. Her plays—*Twilight, Los Angeles* (1992) and *Fires in the Mirror* (1993)—framed conflict in the very communities I had lived in as a child or where I had studied in graduate school. In summer 2006, Sarah Jones would explore the diverse voices of immigrants in Queens, New York, with her Broadway smash hit *Bridge and Tunnel.*

But my role model in feminist theatre was Lily Tomlin, whose one-woman show *The Search for Signs of Intelligent Life in the Universe,* written by her partner Jane Wagner, opened on Broadway in 1985. I saw that show when I was 24, and my friends and I were personally invited to meet Lily backstage. When I wrote to her afterwards, expressing how much that extra attention meant to us, she wrote back immediately, enclosing an autographed photo and a loving note for me.

My next role models in one-woman theatre would be the actresses and comics I met at women's music festivals, venues hosting the very best of feminist theatre during the 1970s, '80s, and '90s. I worked at a dozen different festivals after graduate school, and was fortunate to know some of the best storytellers in the country: jazz vocalist Rhiannon, who spoke as a Scandinavian immigrant mother on the prairies of nineteenth-century South Dakota; Marga Gomez, who recreated her showman father in *A Line Around the Block;* Sherry Glaser, who portrayed all of her own Jewish relatives in the one-woman show *Family Secrets;* Sherry Hicks, whose *Phoenix the* (staged in both voice and American Sign Language) explored her life growing up as the hearing child of Deaf adults. The list goes on and on: Jude Narita, Carolyn

Brandy, Jeanette Buck, Amy Ziff, and many more all created autobiographical one-woman shows. Seeing strong performers like these each August at the Michigan Women's Music Festival inspired me to tell my own story. After all, no one else seemed to be doing comedy about teaching women's studies, which was a relief, since I can't play guitar.

I had already enjoyed good responses to an earlier performance piece, *Passing*, which drew on my experiences as the not-Jewish-looking daughter of a Jewish mother and a Gentile dad. Filtering my private life through a public stage venue had become familiar and, as with *Passing*, I wrote the *Revenge* script in about two days' time. I wanted to recreate about a dozen actual incidents from my career as humorously as possible—coming across as funny and entertaining was central to disproving the giant stereotype that *feminists have no sense of humor*. I knew from personal experience that many women's studies departments had no budget for bringing in guest speakers or booking the main theatre venues on their own campuses, so I wrote *Revenge* as an easily staged event lasting exactly an hour, and my publicity materials made it clear that I could do the show comfortably in a classroom, a church basement, a large living room, a gym, or (as later happened) in the ballroom of a ship as it steamed toward the Straits of Gibraltar. All I needed was a chair. Loud since birth, I've never needed a microphone. And I didn't expect to make any money with this thing: Usually I'd ask if a sponsoring school could cover my travel costs and find a bed for me to crash on in somebody's home. No limo treatment or suite at the Wyndham; I'm not Dame Judi Dench. Maybe a bottle of spring water? By asking for so little, I presented a cost-effective choice for a Women's History Month program at many schools. My international presentations of *Revenge* were usually arranged after I already had travel plans in order and knew I'd be in Dublin or Reykjavik for a week. I'd simply contact the local women's studies program office and offer to stop by with a guest presentation, free of charge. This had the added bonus of guaranteeing my introduction to movers and shakers in the local feminist community, and if I passed the hat after my show I'd glean enough in donations to go out to dinner with my hosts.

Despite my background in theatre, appearing in plays and musicals since age 11, I definitely quaked at taking certain risks in impersonating my own students or "voicing" other roles. Beyond characterization, there was the initial labor of memorizing fifteen single-spaced pages of script. Every show always left me hungry for at least two meals; that's my *life* I'm retelling, the insults and triumphs of a long career, with the question-and-answer period afterwards often longer and more dramatic than the performance itself.

One reason I wanted to tour with a play about women's studies stereotypes was because I don't "look like" Jerry Falwell's image of a feminist. I'm an eyeliner-wearing femme like my flamboyant Jewish mother, Myra. (I did stop shaving my legs for a while in graduate school—until my father offered to loan me the lawnmower.) The hairy-legged, masculine stereotype associated with women's studies professors does still apply to the current chair of my program at George Washington University: He's a man, the esteemed and wonderful Dan Moshenberg.

But the most common, negative image in our society, the one that scares everyone, is that a women's studies professor is *angry.* I was determined to change that by introducing myself as a cheerful, upbeat, approachable soul with a friendly face. I shamelessly made the most of my all-American surfergirl looks, smiling and putting audiences at ease. And then, just when they relaxed, I raised the uncomfortable issues we all need to address.

From Israel to Iceland, from India to Ireland, from New Zealand to Canada, and from Duke University to the Crazy Ladies Bookstore in Cincinnati, I've spent fifteen years talking to student, faculty, and community groups about why there's so much hatred toward women's studies. Does it simply reflect the hatred toward women embedded in most cultures? A society with distaste for women will show distaste for women's studies, assigning low status to both. Audiences in Tel Aviv, Chennai, Dublin, Kentucky, and Ontario all reported *the same* experiences: students being mocked for choosing a women's studies major, threatened by their husbands or boyfriends, accused of witchcraft and lesbianism just for enrolling in a night course tailored to working mothers. The global pattern is undeniable: Women interested in what happens to women are called perverts. And serious scholars of women's history spend as much time defending their chosen field as they do pursuing important research. The old saying "Whatever doesn't kill you makes you stronger" certainly applies to this crowd, but should any first-time college student have to be made to feel she's a threat to the family simply for studying the *history* of the family?

Clearly, there's work to be done.

The following chapters break down my actual, hour-long play script into the ten scenes you'd normally see onstage. I've built a chapter around each scene, explaining what led me to write that portion. I've included a few old photos and posters, too; and yes, I'm still available to set up a show for your community or campus. But let's start at the beginning, when the play opens, back when I was a kid in Durham, North Carolina. After all, how does a kid decide to become a women's studies professor?

1.

Scene One, 1973
My First Women's Studies Class

I'm 12 years old and I've become a feminist. I'm taking my first women's studies class, and every month I read *Ms.* magazine from cover to cover. I want to know more about the women's movement! I think it's so cool that Shirley Chisholm ran for president; if only I was old enough to vote!

I go to a Quaker School, a Friends School, where boys can take dance and girls can learn carpentry; it's the first racially integrated school in the county, too. We call our teachers by their first names: the principal is Don, and he's married to Darlene, who started teaching Women's Studies in the middle school last spring. Don told me I should think about taking Darlene's upper school class; that I should be learning with the high school girls. I don't even have my period yet. My mind is growing faster than all my other parts put together. This can be embarrassing. I said I'd think about it.

When I signed up for the upper school course on feminism, Don passed me in the library with a big smile and said, "I hear you've joined the 'Women' crowd." It's nice to have him support me! He told me I should write books, too, someday!

So now me and my best friend, Jennifer, are the only middle school girls in the class. The rest are older upper school girls,

OPPOSITE PAGE: Age 16, 1977, campaigning for the ERA. This "God is a woman" t-shirt raised eyebrows everywhere. PHOTO BY CHRISTOPHER ROSSE.

all fully developed with long straight hair or big shiny Afros.
Sometimes I'm scared of them. I mean, most of them can drive.

Our assignment for fall 1973 is to write a fifteen-page paper
on a woman we admire and to prepare a dramatic reading about
the 1848 Seneca Falls Women's Rights Convention. I'm learning
that many Quaker women, like Lucretia Mott, became feminists
while opposing slavery; Lucretia and her friend Elizabeth Cady
Stanton went to a World Anti-Slavery conference in London
and were denied entry just because they were women. Even
the most important abolitionist men, back then, said, "No Girls
Allowed." As if they were running a treehouse, not a conference
to end slavery. As if girls and women weren't slaves, too.

So we all practice our lines and then present our dramatic
reading at the downtown YWCA. I'm so excited I throw up in the
parking lot. But I get myself together and play my role; they even
put an article about us in the paper. It's on the "Women's Page,"
with all the recipes, but I don't care. People came and listened
to us! They applauded! Telling women's history is what I want
to do forever. And public speaking ought to be a lot easier, and I
ought to look and sound a lot better, once I get my braces off.

This is the opening scene of *Revenge,* and like the other play scenes to
follow, it's a true story; one that shows how early encouragement really does
determine one's future. My first women's studies teachers handed me the con-
nection between women's history and public storytelling by putting me on
stage—in the role of nineteenth-century suffragist Martha Wright—in 1973,
when I was 12.

At that time, the early 1970s, second-wave feminism was everywhere you
looked. Women's studies programs and women's history courses were emerging across the United States, from the most sheltered of Catholic women's
colleges to the longest-running masters program on women and public policy
at George Washington University, where I teach today. By 1974 the Feminist Press in New York had published a guide entitled *Who's Who and Where
in Women's Studies,* edited by Tamar Berkowitz, Jean Mangi, and Jane Williamson, with an introduction by Florence Howe; it listed more than 4,658
courses being taught in U.S. colleges. Howe noted, "Of the more than 2000
colleges and universities in the country, 885 are listed in this volume as offering women's studies courses. One hundred and twelve of these institutions

offer women's studies programs, approximately a third of which are degree-granting." Only one school, however, offered a Ph.D. in women's history at that time: the State University of New York at Binghamton (endearingly misspelled "Binghampton" in the book's introduction). Nine years later, I would enroll in that program.

Who's Who and Where in Women's Studies offers a fantastic look at the range of scholarship available to new women's studies students in the 1972–74 era: from courses like Women and the Law at Rutgers University (taught by future Supreme Court Justice Ruth Bader Ginsburg) to Women in Cross-Cultural Perspectives at MIT, Women in Literature and Media at UCLA, and Sex Discrimination, Employment, and Family Life at small Mount St. Mary's. Rather than shying away from the controversies of feminist theory, religious colleges for women embraced the opportunity for an open dialogue on women in Church law. Traditionally Catholic and conservative Boston College offered no fewer than six courses on feminist theology, religion, and ethics, taught by outspoken Church critic Mary Daly; St. Joseph's College in Brooklyn offered A History of Women's Liberation in the 19th and 20th Centuries, taught by Sister J. D. Halon and Sister H. Ceborski. Georgetown University, a Jesuit campus that had only recently admitted women as full-time undergraduates, offered four seminars on sex discrimination and law—as well as a course called Women's and Men's Liberation.

But few such courses were available in high schools, where information about women's bodies and "women's problems" (including pregnancy and abortion) remained tightly censored. It would be years before a modest Women's History Month joined the calendar, bringing facts on foremothers into the K–12 curriculum. And while college courses in women's history represented an enormous breakthrough, bear in mind that during the early seventies many women still did not expect to go to college. Ivy League campuses admitted women with reluctance and resistance—Harvard had a quota system of 2.5 males for every female accepted. No athletic scholarships existed for girls. And even the most gifted female students, those who knew they were college-bound, were kept in their place by attitudes and warnings about the proper conduct of ladies. I experienced this first-hand.

When my family moved to North Carolina in the early 1970s, I was a bright 10-year-old who scored high on I.Q. tests and had the opportunity to skip a grade or two. In my new public school, I placed into the E.T. class, shorthand for "exceptionally talented." But on the first day of sixth grade, our teacher told this classroom of hand-picked "gifted" girls, "I do not believe in Women's Lib. There are things boys are able to do, and things girls are able to do, and you will be kept separate as much as possible." My teacher was in clear violation of Title IX, which had become law the previous spring, and which guaranteed that no education opportunity be denied students in federally funded schools on account of sex. She spoke those words about the proper limitations on girls during the autumn of 1972, when Shirley Chisholm, an African American woman, was running for president of the United States. I knew about Chisholm's campaign because my mother took me to hear her speak; I had her poster on my bedroom wall.

The majority of my classmates' parents were professors at Duke or UNC–Chapel Hill, part of the elite Research Triangle. We all expected to go to college ourselves; to my knowledge, at least six out of the ten girls in that one class later became doctors or professors. Yet the message handed to us on that first day of school in 1972, two months after the passage of Title IX, was clear: Girls aren't equal. Know your place.

When I caused trouble by challenging these rules, one of the E.T. teachers told my mother I should be whipped with a paddle. Although my parents were not wealthy, they felt they had no choice but to find a private school for me.

This was how I happened to enroll at Carolina Friends School, an educational institution that changed my life—and the lives of countless other lucky, lucky kids. There, we were encouraged to proceed at our own pace in any field we liked; gender was no barrier. Class discussions on the new women's liberation movement were supported by the faculty and divided into age-appropriate seminars: one section for the middle school (ages 10–13), another for the upper school girls (14–18). The younger group focused on attitudes toward the female body in health, medicine, and media; they used the newly released book *Our Bodies, Ourselves,* published by the Boston Women's Health Collective. Because the book contained frank discussions of reproduction and sexuality, only students with a responsibility rating of 5—the Carolina Friends School equivalent of being A+, mature, and reliable—could enroll. "Women" was notorious for being the only middle school class restricted in this way to the most serious of students. Years later, some CFS graduates and I debated why the younger students looked at biology and sexuality while the older group studied women's history; shouldn't it have been the other way around? No, said several (and I agreed); the 12-year-olds going through puberty needed to study the reproductive system; the older girls were studying suffrage because they were preparing to graduate and vote.

By the way, our class on suffrage included a 13-year-old male student,

York, the son of our women's studies teacher and artist Peggy Phelps. York, ever Mr. Cool, had no objections to playing a female role (suffragist Jane Hunt) in our Seneca Falls drama at the YWCA. Although I frequently played a boy onstage in drama class productions, I had not considered that a boy might be cast as a girl. Another awakening!

Everything about that first women's history class set my career in motion. I can recall sitting under my mother's ancient, space-helmet-style hair dryer, eating oven-cooked Tater Tots, desperately perfecting a long term paper on Florence Nightingale and her emergence as a battlefield nurse. I remember a Saturday morning rehearsal of the Seneca Falls script in Don and Darlene's living room, aware that the school principal himself had cheerfully turned his house into a safe space for teenage feminists to meet. We were held to tough academic standards in that class (a fifteen-page paper), but we made our fore-mothers' history come alive by staging a public reading.

That same fall, on September 20, 1973, Billie Jean King defeated Bobby Riggs in three straight sets, putting the women's sports revolution in motion. The equal rights amendment had passed both the U.S. Senate and the House of Representatives. The braces came off my teeth; my period arrived; I was a young woman at last, and moved out of the room I'd shared with my younger brother, into my own space. There I began a journal, which I've kept through-out my life. I came of age as a woman along with the women's movement.

When I look back at that year, and that first classroom, I'm struck by how readily we girls did identify as women. Barely teenagers, we strongly reso-nated with "women's issues," understanding that we'd be female all our lives and had a lifelong investment in overturning state-sanctioned discrimination. We embraced the word *woman* as a symbol of power and respect, confront-ing adult men who referred to their secretaries or personal assistants as "the girl," and challenging (especially there in the south) white men and women who referred to their housekeepers, often elderly black women, as "the girl." The rejection of *girl* had a lot to do with challenging attitudes of exclusion or belittlement: treehouses with signs that said "No Girls Allowed," boys and coaches who jeered, "You throw like a girl" as the ultimate insult. We were also aware of antifeminist literature like Marabel Morgan's book *The Total Woman*, which urged wives' complete submissiveness to their husbands and addressed them condescendingly as "girls."

That rallying cry, the word *woman*, was inseparable from second-wave feminism. I fell asleep at night to Helen Reddy's "I Am Woman" on radio WDNC, WSSB, WQDR, WCHL. A central focus of the 1970s was simply granting adult women the same rights adult men enjoyed: the right to get a credit card, open a bank account, tee off on a golf course, apply for a job. Girlhood was a temporary status, ending at 18; but with increasing longevity in a health-conscious America, we'd be women for another fifty or sixty years after that. The phrase "women and children" as a mark of chivalry revealed that in most cultures throughout history, adult women had no more rights than minors in the eyes of the law. For all these reasons, the women's movement of the 1970s discouraged adult women from calling themselves "girls." And, at 12 going on 13, watching my Jewish friends have their Bar or Bat Mitzvah, I was fascinated that my own culture named me a woman at 12. Jewish boys matured later; by tradition, they did not recite "Today I am a man" until they turned 13.

This history is significant because today, when I teach Introduction to Women's Studies here in the nation's capital, I find very few college students willing to identify as women. And even fewer have had the luxury of taking a women's history class in high school, let alone middle school. What caused such a change? What's different now?

First of all, I'm 46—the same age, or older, than my students' moms. Every generation sees its parents as old-fashioned or unhip, if not embarrassingly retro. Some of my students were raised by mothers inspired, like me, by 1970s feminism; the students naturally associate "women's issues" with that older/parent generation. Feminism is—or was—Mom's historical moment; and, like Charleston-dancing flappers or the Cold War, it belongs to a specific era. Worse, feminism has been inextricably linked, by an unkind media, with badly dressed public harridans—at best, PTA mothers from hell, and at worst, whining victims and the killer lesbian karate experts who defend them. What could the political issues of the women's movement possibly have to do with freewheeling, belly-pierced college sophomores? (For aging women's studies professors, it can be painful to acknowledge that our own young adult years *are* historically distant.)

Second, a surprising number of students keenly resent the gains of the women's movement because they feel their career-oriented moms were not around as much as they wished. As always, this debate over working vs. stay-at-home moms marginalizes those students whose single or working-class mothers had to hold jobs, whether they yearned to be at home or not. More affluent students who believe that 1970s feminism invented the working mother get a wake-up call from classmates who quickly defend their own parents' sacrifices. Often it is the son of a working single mom who speaks up most eloquently in a women's studies classroom.

Finally, there is the discomfort with the word *woman*. Somewhere along the line, in the 1990s, American culture shifted from empowering women to empowering girls, and this explosion of "girl" slogans and material culture is well documented in Jennifer Baumgardner and Amy Richards' book *Manifesta* (2000). Reclaiming "girl" had a generational push from new young activists weary of being lectured on sexist word usage. During a recent retrospective on the Riot Grrrl music movement which sprang up during the early 1990s, Allison Wolfe from Bratmobile recalled: "I'd be taking women's studies classes and whenever I'd use the term *girl*, everyone would turn around and correct me, hissing, *woman*. But I was 19! I identified as a girl." Irritation with being shamed about language led some frustrated young feminists to stick with girl power—or grrrl power.

Girl power offers a range of choices—from "cute" girliness to the more pungent attitudes of Riot Grrrl rock or the "Girls Kick Ass" sports pride spiraling outward from Title IX and the 1999 World Cup soccer victory. Girl power is also used interchangeably with *women* to make political feminism seem cuddlier, less negative: as in this editorial from the publisher of *BUST* magazine: "Of course, we devote space in our pages to typical 'feminist issues' . . . but we're also determined to create a truly embraceable women's culture, so that reading *BUST* can help you feel good about being a girl."[1] *Girly*, alas, is still being used as an insult by men in power, primarily to demean other males: In 2004, California governor Arnold Schwarzenegger made the notorious slur *girlymen* against his liberal opponents.

Part of the appeal in choosing *girl* over *woman* is the postponement of adult choices and responsibilities. More than ever before, young women are in college, far outnumbering male classmates at institutions across the country. Marriage? Having a baby? That's all put off until later—not due to any strident feminist convictions but in order to get a B.A., an M.A., an internship, and then a first job to pay off those student loans, all while making ends meet by still living at home. . . . A *woman* is independent; has finished all of that preliminary young-adult stuff. She's met her spouse; owns a home. She's ready for motherhood.

Facing my new classes each semester, I remind myself that most students are starting their scholarly journey into gender history at 19 or 20, not 12. Many, if not all, have already been sexually active for years, trying to make informed decisions about birth control, sexual harassment, or abortion with-

---

1. Debbie Stoller, Editorial, *BUST* (Oct./Nov. 2006): 6.

out knowing how other women have negotiated these issues throughout history. Too many of my students are already survivors of date rape. But they've yet to talk about the politics of womanhood *during school;* throughout their educations, what happens to women has been improper subject matter, all but banned from the K–12 learning environment. Puberty may begin at age 10 for many American girls, but for the next eight years they're subjected to abstinence-only sex ed classes, which prevent direct answers to tough questions in class. Being treated like a child, at 17, is poor preparation for identifying as a woman at 18.

"How many of you think of yourselves as women?" I ask a group of twenty-five stylish, accomplished Georgetown students; not a single arm flies up. Most of these students are 21, interns for congresswomen on Capitol Hill, scholarship athletes directly benefiting from Title IX. In every way but one—the ongoing ban on women as priests, at historically Jesuit Georgetown—they see women in limitless positions of power, strength, and decision-making. They're grateful for the feminist activists who helped broaden the scope of opportunities available to them. In their eyes, however, feminism belongs to their mothers' generation, the tacky 1970s. They're not ready to identify with their mothers. Their moms are women. They're not.

"Let's put it another way. When do you think girls become women in American society today?" is my next question. And that's when responses pour out.

It seems unfair that we only get thirteen years of girlhood while the remaining seventy will be spent as women. It's a work in progress. Eventually, I'll make that full transition. Until then, I guess you could call me a pre-woman.

Girls are wearing tight jeans, belly shirts, and makeup at younger ages, swearing, getting used to male attention. I see older men ogling girls in miniskirts and tank tops who can't be over 15 years old.

My time finally came! At last, I felt worthy of adult status! We walked to the toiletries aisle, and I picked out a pearl white razor with purple detailing, rushed home, and got down to business. Half an hour later, both legs shaved, I was officially a woman.

The day I noticed my breasts I had no idea what to do with them.

I'm stuck on the notion that one is not a woman until she wears suits and walks to work in black hose and white sneakers with her pumps held together in her hand.

I only realized the importance of my first period when I overheard my mother crying on the phone with her own mother, saying, "I've lost my little girl." That was so private. I needed something very public. The day I became a woman was the March for Women's Lives in Washington, D.C., in April 2004.

Parents say "You need to grow up," but at the same time, "You're growing up way too fast." So could someone please calculate the rate of how fast I should grow up?

I have just reached the age my mother was when she got pregnant with me. And it startled me; hell, it downright scared me! I had a fish in fall semester, and it died. I killed a fish in two weeks, and people my age have children?

As terrible as it sounds, womanhood is something I dread. Grown-up women are conservative, moody, and tired. They have varicose veins, and drive mini-vans. I don't want to give up sports for cooking dinner, or my midriff t-shirts for floral-printed sweaters. Grown women are forced to step aside for the hottest, up-and-coming 16-year-old.

My friend had a quinceañera. She wore a glorious ball gown and tiara and performed a choreographed waltz. But toward the end of the evening her focus shifted from cultural pride in becoming a woman to anxiety over when she could open her gifts. When her father reprimanded her for spending more time with her gifts than her guests, she began crying like a little kid. Those gifts had an opposite effect. Instead of congratulating her on becoming a woman, they just revealed her childishness.

I grew up in the Bible Belt of America, where one is always a lady, female sexuality is taboo, and white dresses rule each stage of life. But I stand firm in my opinion that a white dress does not a woman make.

My sister is about to turn 15. She said, "You become a woman the first time that someone tells you that you are beautiful."

My mom said, "Really strong relationships with
other women is part of becoming a woman."

I hope one day to repeat the words of Mrs. Durant, who
I see at the beauty salon. She is 82 years old and told
me she is "still becoming a woman every day."

I believe my coming-of-age ceremony did not occur at
my Bat Mitzvah, but when I wanted to spend an entire
day with my mother. That was my rite of passage.

I remember the first time I was actually whistled at on the street, at
age 14. I felt both exhilarated to receive that kind of attention—and
disgusted, sexually objectified. It opened my eyes to the harsh
reality that as a woman, I would be constantly viewed as an object.

The first time a girl realizes she is a woman is when she
begins to hate, dislike or distrust her own body.

Here at Georgetown female students are called "college girls." On
the other hand, girls that do not attend college after high school and
instead find a job and live on their own become "working women."

This last comment offers great insight; college extends youthful playtime
for a few more years, and students at elite colleges are aware of this privileged,
sheltered time in their lives. Once they've graduated and are earning a living,
no longer dependent on their parents, then they'll be women and men. But
plenty of my Georgetown and GWU students plan to go to graduate school,
too, some of them still living at home or otherwise supported by parents' tuition dollars. When will womanhood come for them? One student had it all
figured out:

If for whatever reason a female continues to live at home, is solely
dependent on her parents, and has no responsibilities, she does
ultimately by default become a woman at around the age of 30.

Such women were, not too long ago, pitied as "spinsters." Life was over
for them, unmarried at 30. Now we take for granted that with a longer life
expectancy, adulthood is just starting at 30—with degrees and internships

finally completed, the confidence of womanhood can finally emerge. The uncertainty and lack of confidence marking young women's long, long adolescence in American culture became a joke on the television series *Rhoda* in the mid-1970s: Instead of a theme song, that sitcom introduced actress Valerie Harper declaring before each episode: "I had a bad puberty. It lasted seventeen years."

So here we are, in the first decade of the twenty-first century, where one is a girl at 29, and womanhood is deferred as long as possible. If it was different for me—eager to examine women's issues at 12—and different for my mother, whose Jewish community in 1950s Los Angeles urged girls to look and dress like little adults at 15 in preparation for a good marriage—how much more different it was for women and girls in the past! And so I begin the semester by assigning books like Marilyn Yalom's *A History of the Wife,* or Sarah Pomeroy's *Goddesses, Whores, Wives and Slaves,* or Mary Odem's *Delinquent Daughters.* What did *girl* or *woman* mean in ancient Greece, where a girl married at 12 a man of 30 or more, and remained a perpetual minor in the eyes of the law? How would abstinence until marriage apply to female slaves in antebellum America, whose marriages to male slaves were unrecognized in U.S. law and who could, as property, be raped by their owners for the purpose of incubating more slaves? Why was the age of consent as low as 7, in Delaware, in 1870?

In a land clamoring for a return to "traditional family values," have traditional societies ever truly protected women and their children? Author Jane Smiley notes, "My daughter, who is twenty-six, wishes American feminism had produced a society like Norway or Sweden, where child rearing and family life are considered the business of the entire country. . . . Where good prenatal care, breast-feeding, excellent day care, good medical care, anti-child abuse laws and programs, and proper educational facilities are considered the rights of all rather than the privilege of a few. . . . American feminism has failed indeed, because it has failed to promote the common good of women and children."[2]

This is the conversation few of us are prepared to have, the one that I begin with every autumn; the simple hazards of surviving *girlhood.*

---

2. Jane Smiley, "Feminism Meets the Free Market," in *The Mommy Wars,* ed. Leslie Steiner (New York: Random House, 2006), 204.

**Northern Kentucky University Women's Studies Program
& Crazy Ladies Bookstore proudly present:**

Dr. Bonnie Morris

in an original One Woman Play:

REVENGE
of the Women's Studies Professor

**Tuesday, November 14
7:30 p.m. University Center Theater
Highland Heights Campus**

Admission: $3

(Women's Studies students may attend free)

❖ ❖ ❖

- What is it like to pursue Women's Studies as a teaching career?
- How do students, administrators, and complete strangers react to the feminist scholar?
- This one-woman play presents a behind the scenes look at real incidents and challenges--some funny, some painful, in the early stages of one feminist professor's career.

For Tickets or More information contact Crazy Ladies Bookstore at
(513)541-4198.
Ticket sales & donations support the Crazy Ladies Bookstore.

Ad for a benefit performance in Cincinnati, 1995

2.

Scene Two, 1983
You're Getting a Ph.D. in *What*?

I'm all grown up now, and I've graduated summa cum
laude from American University. I'm proud to be the first
AU student to graduate with a minor in women's studies,
and now I'm heading off to graduate school in Binghamton,
New York, to earn a Ph.D. in women's history.

Everywhere I go, I tell people—friends, relatives, strangers—
about my work and my ambitions. My goal is to be a professor,
and some people think that's great. But through six long years
of grad school, this is what I hear from everyone else:

"You're working on a Ph.D. in what?!"
"Women's history. This is a field?"
"I didn't know you could major in women's lib.
God, how disgustingly politically correct."
"Think you're going to earn any money with that?"
"You'll never get a job. You'll have to go on
welfare. You'll be a drain on society."
"I was in World War II. I was in a submarine.
Now, that's history, missy!"

I'm astounded by how hostile complete strangers are. Is
everyone truly concerned that I might have a hard time getting a
tenured job? Or are they flabbergasted that, at 22, I am pursuing
exactly what I want to do instead of a more conventionally feminine
career? It would never occur to me to mock someone's chosen
profession to their face, especially when being introduced to them

for the first time. But over and over again, this happens to me, at the oddest places. Like the time I attend an old friend's engagement party. She presents me to her handsome fiancé, saying, "This is Bonnie—she's writing a dissertation on Jewish women's history." And he looks me up and down and snorts, "And you expect to be employable?" How tempted I am to rub cake in his face!

Ah, but I survive. I hang on. And every so often, there are nice comments, too, from strangers. Like the time I sit next to a successful businesswoman on a long airplane flight. She sees me grading papers and asks what work I do. When I explain that I study the history of women, she grins and leans in closer. "So," she whispers. "How are we doing?"

This is the scene that really resonates with young women's studies students. How *do* we countenance derision toward our work throughout long years of study? Few people will praise us for choosing the subject Women. What does that say about our world? Are there effective techniques for dealing with unprompted rudeness? How does one prepare for a lifetime of serving as a diplomat from the land of scholarly feminism?

Here in America, we are a rude society; and, alas, growing ruder every year, in no small part due to the uncivil tone of political debate. The so-called culture wars have us hurling names at one another, and too often women are cast in the worst possible roles. I've already mentioned the epithet *feminazis;* before that there was Phyllis Schlafly's book *The Power of the Positive Woman,* which offered us the phrase *femlib fanatics.* Women who support reproductive rights and legal abortion are *babykillers,* and, in too much of rap and hip hop, we hear strong women reduced to *bitches* and *hoes.* Then there's the daily reminder that all women are mere genitalia. "Don't be a pussy," I hear men admonish one another nearly every single day. Stripped of its sheer sexual connotation, *pussy* means weakling, rather ironic when one considers the astounding physical capacity (thirty-six hours of labor, anyone?) of that vaginal mother-portal through which men enter the world. But the woman as body is nasty, weak, corrupt, sinful, evil.

A life spent on women's issues? A career built on women's history? So many strangers feel free to tell me that's a waste, a perversion, unprofitable, worthless. *Worth less.*

But if, by age 17 or 18, we have learned to deal with anatomical name-calling, we can surely learn to deal with slurs on our chosen professions,

studies, majors. I knew, before graduating from high school, that in college
I wanted to study women's history and possibly major or minor in a related
field, and the summer before I entered American University in Washington,
D.C., I accepted a job going door to door fundraising for the equal rights
amendment. This proved to be excellent preparation for the insults I'd endure
over time as a feminist and as a publicly identifiable activist. I learned, then,
to endure stranger-rudeness on a massive scale, and to turn specific verbal
attacks on women's worth into material for my own writing, college papers,
and lecture presentations.

Question: Who remembers the equal rights amendment? Fervent national debate over its merits defined my coming of age in the late 1970s. "Equality of rights under the law shall not be denied by the United States or by any
state on account of sex." The amendment, first introduced by suffragist Alice
Paul in 1923, was actually endorsed first by the Republican Party in 1940 and
then by the Democratic Party in 1944, winning President Truman's support
at the end of World War II (perhaps in recognition of American women's
contribution to the war effort—much as historians suggest the Nineteenth
Amendment passed in acknowledgment of women's sacrifices during World
War I). Decades later, Congress finally passed the ERA in 1972 and ushered
in an agonizing decade of state-by-state ratification. Six states ratified within
two days (Hawaii was first) but only thirty-three of the required thirty-eight
states had ratified by 1974—the year that the John Birch Society and Phyllis
Schlafly's Eagle Forum declared the amendment to be a Communist plot and
began a highly successful STOP ERA campaign. With thirty-five states in tow
by 1977, the year of the well-attended National Women's Conference in Texas,
only three states were needed—and the deadline for their ratification was extended to 1982. Hope focused on Illinois, Florida—and North Carolina. The
clock was ticking.

It was a cliffhanger of a time, a perfect time to hone debate skills as a
young political activist. At 16 and 17, still taking women's studies courses at
Carolina Friends School, I knew where I stood: with feminism. I attended
school wearing a t-shirt with the exact wording of the ERA printed across my
chest. My classmates and I, brainy girls all, National Merit semi-finalists and
college achievement test whizzes, were being deluged with letters from prestigious universities: *Pick us! Apply to us!* Yet each morning, anti-ERA letters
and editorials appearing in local and national newspapers trumpeted derision for the very idea of equality. We were graduating into a society that still
believed even the most talented girls were not equal to the least worthy boys.
I felt I was back in that sixth-grade classroom with the teacher who intoned,

"There are only some things girls can do." I was graduating from a more enlightened school, but in a state that had failed to ratify the ERA. This mixed message—that I might be outstanding academically, in the top 1 percent of the nation, but I should expect second-class treatment under the law—sent me into the streets. At the state capitol in Raleigh, North Carolina, pro- and anti-ERA groups clashed during rallies in that spring of 1979. I was poked in the belly with a Confederate flag. My then-boyfriend, the Jewish son of a Holocaust survivor, got a different kind of painful poke for showing support of my rights: "Son," an angry woman confronted him, "What's wrong with you? Aren't you a Christian?"

Attending a Quaker school, we were surrounded daily by men and women who had taken far worse verbal and physical violence for participating in racial integration of the south. Our teachers—stalwart civil rights veterans like Cal Geiger, who had worked for the American Friends Service Committee—were living legacies of technique and philosophy in nonviolent resistance. Turning the other cheek when hounded by opponents, they modeled a very different sort of activism. These were lessons I internalized that proved helpful in handling all sorts of anti-feminist backlash—whether rhetorical or physical.

So, when I needed a summer job to earn money before starting college, I took a paid position as a door-to-door canvasser for the Women's Resources E.R.A. Fund at the National Women's Political Caucus. Throughout the summer of 1979, I knocked on doors in one of the most powerful and affluent districts of the United States: Montgomery County, Maryland. Fresh from a loving, supportive, private alternative school, I felt as raw as two skinned knees when I saw how hostile many congressmen were to the promise of women's rights.

All fundraisers get their share of abuse knocking on doors regardless of the organization they represent; even Girl Scouts can be chased away by impatient homeowners who resent being interrupted during dinner or leisure time after work. But my knock on the door forced unwelcome discussion of a truly divisive issue in that time period, and, as an inexperienced teenager looking the part of a classic "treehugger" with my Birkenstocks and long unraveling braid, I was an easy target for adult males' rage toward encroaching feminist change. Even in neighborhoods that were home to many a senator, I experienced threats and curses. I wasn't selling Girl Scout cookies. I was selling equality.

Each day we met at our downtown office, divided into crews, and then piled into station wagons and headed out to the suburbs with our street maps and clipboards. The first house of the day was the hardest. I'd survey its exterior for telltale political clues: car bumper stickers, religious symbols, or (never a good sign) a ceramic slave. I had to adapt my entire pitch to these outward cues as I advanced toward the doorbell.

"Hi! My name is Bonnie Morris, and I'm with the National Women's Political Caucus. We're working to ratify the equal rights amendment and would love to have your signature of support and a tax-deductible donation." By the time I paused for air, the worst was over. At that point, the person who opened the door either interrupted me with a bitter tirade against feminism, or offered me a drink of water and then opened their checkbook.

When I met ERA opponents, I seized the opportunity to educate—in as many languages as I could muster (high school Spanish, elementary Hebrew, the alphabet of American Sign Language). Great confusion and ignorance about the exact wording of the amendment prevailed, even in the best-educated homes. *Equality of rights under the law shall not be denied or abridged by the United States or by any state on account of sex.* It was right there on my t-shirt and clipboard. But no matter how often I recited the words, people still refused to believe it stopped there. If that was the language, what was all the fuss about? Wasn't it really about . . . shared bathrooms?

"So, where's the part about the co-ed bathrooms?" women asked me every single day. "Where's the part you're not showing me, about the forced abortions and everyone becoming homosexuals?"

"No, ma'am, it's just about equality," I tried. And then some housewives said to me, "But I'm not equal to any man, sweetheart. And neither are you."

"It's people like *you* who are ruining this country!" shrieked one man, forbidding me to approach his wife, who cowered in the shadows of a long hallway. Others cheerfully commanded their dogs to chase me out of the driveway: *Rex! Rover! Get the little feminist!* Some men laughed through my equality sales pitch, then propositioned me for sex. An elderly woman put a curse on me; another shook her fist as I approached and hissed, "Don't even talk to me; I detest you people." And still others offered me drugs—or the Bible. Cocaine or Proverbs 31 would take care of my unfulfilled soul, these homeowners promised.

An irate husband ordered me out of his yard. He declared his own opposition to equal rights, and I dared to ask if this was also his wife's opinion: Could I speak to the woman of the house, please? "You'd better not, young lady," he screamed between clenched teeth, moving toward me, and that was one time when I felt fairly afraid and skedaddled on to the next house. But a curious thing happened. This couple's young son, a boy of 6 who had observed all of this wide-eyed, tugged at his father's pants leg and said over and over, "But Dad, what if Mom knows something about this? Huh? What if Mom knows?"

Asking Mom to cast her own, separate ballot was still a radical act in 1979, fifty-nine years after the Nineteenth Amendment passed into law. The old view that the man of the house spoke for Mom, and controlled her legally, was familiar to me from my first women's studies classes on the suffrage movement. But I met women worn down by struggle, or bound to religious ideals of male headship, who also spoke coldly to me.

Yes, it was great training for dealing with sexism. Or was it? At 18, I was the next-to-youngest field worker (the youngest was a vivacious 15-year-old who had lied about her age to get the job; I kept her secret). Neither of us ever sought support or sympathy if, during the five hours of door-to-door face time among strangers every day, we were threatened or abused or frightened. There was, probably, support and counseling available if any of us were really attacked; yet there was a stoicism about dealing with "normal" backlash. I sensed that since the big girls—the college graduates—weren't whining, I shouldn't either. I kept quiet, writing about my experiences in my journal. But today, decades later, I know that our fake offhandedness masked a very high turnover rate in that office. Too often, organized feminism has ignored its own message: Any kind of daily gender-based harassment takes its toll. Some workers had recurring nightmares; I broke out in a rash. Yes, daily debriefing might have helped us.

Was I too young for this kind of job? No. At 18, I was legally old enough to vote, have sex, and get married. What surprised me was having adults refer to me as "little girl" at the door: "Honey, there's a little girl here who wants ya to sign something!" a man might call to his wife. I was five-foot-six, broad-shouldered, and weighed 135 pounds. And as a bonus eye-opener, I found that while I might be a "little girl" at the door, I was often mistaken for a prostitute at the bus stop after work. Our office building at 14th and K Streets in the nation's capital was part of a notorious cruising strip after dark; ERA canvassers left work each night just as sex workers began pounding the pavement. This overlap in labor hours had the prostitutes and professional feminists rubbing shoulders in line at the corner fast food joint most nights, as powerful men on their way home from government jobs sized us up. Many nights, waiting for my Metrobus, I was approached and asked if I was for sale: "How much, honey?"

"Make yourself some real money, girlfriend," suggested a tall, thin woman sporting pink boots, a pink parasol—and a black eye. This was before anyone had heard of AIDS.

What I struggled with, that summer, was the sheer unglamorous grunt work involved in attaining social justice. Of course there were bright moments and wonderful encounters with people I met at the door: sculptors, diplomats, clergy, bakers, photographers, bikers in leather, lonely young mothers who showed me their children's crayon drawings. Men and women opened their hearts and wallets, not only donating money but stuffing me with Popsicles, fresh lemonade, cookies, and offers of free kittens. Still, every day I heard angry insults that made me ponder my place as an intelligent woman in a democracy. I saw the most highly educated men in the country slam door after door on the possibility of women's equality. The congressmen I met had attended law school alongside female classmates, learned from at least some female professors, were now raising daughters, and still went on to defeat statutes promising women an equal share in the privileges men enjoyed—hmm. Was it about sharing power, after all?

All that effort—and no ERA. So many of my students, though, think we *have* an equal rights amendment. They're shocked to learn we don't.

Encountering hostility to women's rights from strangers is one thing. I'm used to it by now: from the anti-ERA ranting I endured in the late 1970s to a taxi driver who just yesterday told me, "All women want to be dominated by men; and you are no different, my dear." But students who intend to make women's studies their major can expect ongoing challenges to their work from more intimate acquaintances. How do they develop the patience to talk, really talk, with friends and loved ones and family about why women's history matters? What do they learn, from suspicious boyfriends or parents or roommates, about our society's fear of feminists?

On the first day of any women's studies class I teach, I offer a casual warning: "Someone you care about is going to pick on you for taking this course. We'll be talking about the comments you encounter, and ways to deal with backlash." Within days, students speak up: "My boyfriend and I had a fight about my taking this class. He says that all feminists are . . ."

Here are some effective strategies and personal experiences that students have contributed over the years—in my classes or after my presentations on different campuses.

When I begin any conversation about why I'm a women's studies minor I have to remember that I used to have my own prejudiced images of feminists. It was ingrained in me that whatever else feminism might be, it wasn't good. My best friend in high school educated me. She showed me a world where women who were not psycho man-haters did identify as feminists.

I talked with a freshman I'd never met and feminism came up in the conversation. He suddenly blurted out that we shouldn't speak about it. If feminist issues were discussed, then the "feeling" of our university would disappear; it was as if feminist ideas are part of the angry world and shouldn't invade the cocoon of our protective campus. Most students here come from private schools, and that protection is continued in college; some freshmen I've met here do want to live in a cocoon.

When I first enrolled in gender studies classes, my mother felt so threatened by the prospect that her daughter was now a feminist! She has always felt that the feminist movement was telling her that her choice—to stay home and raise us until we graduated from high school—was worth less. I said that the feminist movement was working to bring respect for all women in whatever job they undertook.

A guy asked me to his fraternity formal, but said if I was going to "talk about the feminist crap from class" not to accept his invitation, as he did not want to be embarrassed in front of all his brothers.

My friend from home, who attends a different college, decided to be a women's studies minor. Her parents refused to pay for the classes, saying they were completely worthless and a waste of time. Her brother, though, attends the same school—and is a history major. He took the one women's studies class cross-listed for history credit, and the parents agreed to pay for it!

I was dumbfounded by comments made by a fellow history major: He snickered about one professor I recommended, saying, "No way. She brings too many women's history issues into class." I asked him if he thought women were a part of history. He replied, "Sure, but you should be able to choose whether or not you have to learn about women's history in a regular history class." I asked what he thought constituted regular history, and he said, "Wars, battles, empires, treaties." I spoke my piece: that society has repeatedly trained its generations to think of history literally in terms of "his story." From the time Americans are young, we teach them that women are not a part of "regular" history—rather, they are secondary, and left by many schools as "elective" studies.

I had an argument in the pub with a male classmate: He found out that I am a women's studies minor. He simply went off his head: I should be shot. Feminists were destroying the economic stability of America by taking jobs away from men. I was going to be a horrible mother and I would never be able to find a husband.

This morning I asked a man in our class why he hasn't been attending. His response was that it made him too angry, listening to some of the things we discuss. It seems that he took the class in hope of discrediting women's studies, but he hasn't been able to dismiss what he is learning—and that's what truly bothers him.

I asked my friends how they liked a certain movie. One remarked, "Well, I don't consider myself a feminist. But it bothered me, the way women were treated back then." I asked her: Why do you need to qualify a dislike for the mistreatment of women? You don't have to be a feminist to realize that the degradation of women is a bad thing. If you see that women are being wrongly treated, even today, and you think maybe something should be done about it, why in hell wouldn't you fight for what you believe in? Is feminism still such a dirty word?

Here's something I deal with from both male and female friends: They think women's studies is just female chauvinism and an excuse for male-bashing. They say, "Why isn't there a men's studies major?" I reply by saying that everything taught in all my other classes is from the male perspective. I ask them: Did they make it past sixth grade without knowing who Benjamin Franklin, Christopher Columbus, or Paul Revere were? Now, at 22, can they recognize Susan B. Anthony? I am only learning who these significant women are because I elected to take a class. Why are women and minorities left out of the history taught to grade school kids, junior high students, and high school students?

When I told my father that I was taking "Feminism in American History," his response was "Oh, Jesus. I thought you were going to take more difficult courses this year. You are still majoring in economics, right?" But when I asked a male friend what he thought of my studying feminism, he said sincerely, "I think that's great! It's definitely a necessary topic to know about, especially for a liberal arts education." Then another male friend responded, "What a waste of time! Feminism is the product of political correctness." I asked, "And what would you say if I told you there are many guys in my class?"

When I told my girlfriend I was taking a women's history class, she said, "Wow, I can't see you as some hardcore feminist." Then she added, "Even though I don't like feminists, I'm glad there are some, because they got things accomplished. Now, hopefully, I'll get a cool job when I enter the working world." I sure wish girls at this school had a better idea of what feminism means!

My mother says that in order to get any major points across to men, especially pertaining to feminist issues, it is necessary to sugarcoat what you say. I subconsciously refrain from saying what's on my mind in front of my male friends because I fear deep down that they will not want to spend time with me. I hate the fact that I censor myself.

When I told my mother I was taking women's history, she was very impressed. But considering her own Ivy League education, she still asked the generic question "So—are you studying about Betsy Ross?" My father, on the other hand, rolled his eyes when I told him about my work in women's history.

I wanted to write my senior history seminar paper on Abigail Adams, and met with my professor to discuss this. But he told me I would be unable to write about Adams because another person in our class had already chosen her and there would not be enough material for both of us. I pointed out that there was no question of there being enough information on John Adams, James Madison, etc. for male students in our group!

This last incident, reported by a star history major at one university where I taught, really made me sit up and take notice. It was a sad reminder that too often, other faculty—including history faculty—are responsible for scornful attitudes toward choosing an academic focus on women. Worried about grades, approval, letters of recommendation, the daily environment of mentoring, few undergraduates want to risk a confrontation with a tenured senior professor about his attitude toward women's history research. But if a pattern emerges over time—if student after student is rebuffed in her quest to do advanced research on women—the university is clearly practicing sex discrimination. And too few students are aware of their rights.

Ultimately, the best way to counter offensive arguments that women's studies classes "don't teach anything" (or only teach man-hating) is to show your critic a copy of the class syllabus. Still, proof of heavy reading loads, multiple-draft term papers, and award-winning scholarly authors won't always satisfy those determined to mock women's history. One of my students showed her boyfriend a copy of our textbook, Aileen Kraditor's classic *Ideas of the Woman Suffrage Movement,* and he refused to open it or even touch it, declaring, "You won't find me reading that crap." For women's studies faculty, this unusual burden—of crafting a course outline intended to defend the subject matter as well as to instruct—begins in graduate school.

My generation, the bridge between the first women's studies professors and the twenty-first-century college students whose mothers were 1970s feminists, often had no institutional forum for discussing how we intended to defend our roles as women's history specialists. Barely out of college ourselves, we signed up, at 21 or 23 or 25, for six years of doctoral training in how to teach the history of our sex. We understood we were privileged to have that choice; the first generation had smoothed the way, and most of the women's historians I met had emerged from that process determined to be as professional as possible. Their radicalism, their intellectual fire, was tempered with conservative dress, discipline of self and others, no-nonsense decorum in the classroom. We were the ones to whom they passed the torch, our grubby hands extended to receive their hard-earned wisdom.

3.

Scene Three, 1986
Exams and Evaluations

Here I am in graduate school, teaching my very first women's history class. My students are a mix of young undergraduates and older married women returning to college. The subject of women in history is something these students never studied in high school, and the books and lectures are confusing to them at first. Real women's history contradicts much of what they were taught about American democracy. They're shocked to learn that many slave women were impregnated by their masters and that white masters often sold their own children for profit. They're amazed that women in the nineteenth century were kept from going to college for fear it would damage their ovaries. They can't believe that female teachers were once required to remain unmarried and childless in order to keep their jobs. "Women's history is all about the law controlling their wombs!" says a mom.

I wait to see how my students handle their first exam. Have they kept up with the readings? What have they learned? How am I doing as a lecturer? I'm only 24.

The night after the exam, subzero winds are howling around my tiny studio apartment, and I curl up under my electric blanket with the stack of blue books and some good cashew nuts. And here is what that first class had to say:

Opposite page: Discovering feminist theatre in graduate school: a 1987 rehearsal at Herizon in Binghamton, New York

Women's history is a lot of individual hairs
that collectively add up to nothing!

Queens just want one thing: to sit upon a thrown.

It was really hard for women in the American
Revolution because there were no phones.

For Comanche women, preparing the food and making
the clothing was not as easy as driving to the mall.

Women nurses in the Civil War had to deal with
unsanitary conditions like filth, chaos, dysentery,
and even litter in their front yard.

Many young immigrant women found it hard to
let go of their parents' old costumes.

After being killed, Brigham Young brought in
the idea of Moronism and polygamy.

Changes in family life included the fact that now
some people lived in the middle of nowhere.

There was a strong bondage between mother and child. But at an
early age, children must be weenied away from the mother's breast.

Most working women were either married or unmarried.

Schoolteachers have come a long way since the Dark Ages.

The women's temperance movement was the attitude that people
shouldn't drink because drunk drinking led to drunkenness.

Society in 1850, after all, was just climbing out of the Middle Ages.

Women found that in America the streets were
not paved in gold—just horse manure.

This was the era of fainting spells, smelling salts and melting beds.

The belles of the South made the men drool,
with their small waists and big butts.

In the 1840s, women began to come out of the closet.

Time after time, the suffragists exposed themselves.

Women's sit-ins were supposed to be peaceful, but
with police dragging people into the paddy wagons,
it sometimes became a very loud scene.

Marriage was one way women relieved themselves.

After World War II, there was a rapid return to the pubic sphere.

Women social workers thought that the main
cause of poor people was poverty.

Women were encouraged to act like the first amphibians,
who climbed out of the primordial slime!

As a matter of fact, there was one famous woman
who was a real woman and stood up to all men.
Unfortunately, I can't remember her name.

I realize then and there that women's studies is just like any other class: We may approach history from a feminist standpoint, but ultimately, it's about clear opening paragraphs, correct grammar, and getting your facts spelled right. Everything after that first exam is put on hold for a week spent on writing and footnoting. No one has a computer or spellcheck yet; it's 1986.

At the end of the semester, after I've turned in my students' grades, I'm allowed to read their course evaluations. I take the stack of comments with interest and fear. I've been friendly but strict. Did they like their first women's history course? Will I make it as a professor? I'm eager to improve; I'll accept their critical feedback on my teaching. But this is what those first evaluations had to say:

Ms. Morris, please shave your legs.

Ms. Morris, quit saying Y'ALL.

Ms. Morris, Jesus loves you.

Ms. Morris, there's too much reading. Please show more movies.

Ms. Morris, please change the time of this class so my
friend can take it. It conflicts with her soap operas.

Ms. Morris, I personally was shocked that you talked

about Freud's theory of the female's organism. Talking
about females having organisms is not professional!

Ms. Morris—my only complaint is that you did not
turn your lovely face more often in my direction.

Every teacher has to start somewhere.

Most audiences enjoy this scene: They can relate to the funny errors so typical of first-year papers, whether they are teachers or students themselves. And they can sympathize with how hopeful and optimistic I was as a new teacher. The scene pokes gentle fun at the thousands and thousands of exams I've graded over time; but it also establishes the women's history classroom as an academic workplace with measurable performance standards. Yes, you can indeed flunk women's studies. It's not an ideological litmus test, either: My right-wing students can earn As, and radical feminists who plagiarize won't pass.

Throughout my career, I have encountered plenty of rude folk who laugh at the very idea of a serious women's history seminar, insisting the subject matter makes it a "Mickey Mouse" course (apologies to Walt Disney). Because of these stereotypes, too many students do show up expecting that women's history will be easy, requiring minimal effort. They're shocked to find that it's just like any other class; indeed, stricter. One young woman burst into tears at first sight of my syllabus and wept, "You mean you expect us to read all that?" before fleeing the classroom, never to return. This academic discipline comes with a double-edged sword: be too friendly, too radical, too circular in the seating arrangements for class discussions, and critics will shout *Aha! Ideological navel-gazing! Mere indoctrination!* But by upholding strict standards of grammar, spelling, punctuation, and historical accuracy, women's studies professors meet a tidal wave of protest—from young women.

"I took this class because I thought it would bring up my grade." "I thought it would be fun; this is just an elective for me—I took it because it fit my workout schedule." "I can't believe you would hurt my grade point average like this—a B on a paper about suffrage will keep me from graduating summa cum laude!" "I fail to see why plagiarism is such a big deal." "You take off so many points for spelling and grammar! This isn't an English class." "You seem to be suggesting that I copied out of the book. As a senior, I am outraged. I merely paraphrased." "I am an A student! By giving me the low grade of B, you have denied me what I deserve."

And then there's the chilling post-feminist phenomenon: women's studies students who cheat. Twice, at George Washington University, I caught an entire women's history class passing around midterm test questions ahead of time; they acquired the exam from a student who took the class previously. No one considered this cheating. But I'm getting ahead of the story.

Putting Together a Strong Syllabus

How does one learn to teach women's history as a subject? At Binghamton (the State University of New York), where I did my graduate work, my colleagues and I took pride in attending a "public Ivy." We were grateful to have been recruited for one of the only Ph.D. programs nationwide with a focus on women's history. No one was there by accident; no one lacked ambition or a work ethic, and the endlessly cold, snowy winters certainly accommodated cuddling up with a few hundred books. As the history department emphasized conducting original research with primary sources, not much time was spent on honing good teaching skills or classroom control. Plunged into teaching assistantships with no preparation, we took our cues from the professors we assisted: noting that this one played to a packed house with all the heart of a stage actor, whereas that one quickly lost students' respect by appearing flustered, and yet another insulted students freely without apparent repercussion or reproval from senior administrators. *Hmmmm*, we thought. *Which one will I be like? Are there any other role models? Is it really kosher to insult students? To teach class drunk? Will I ever gain the chops to lecture as effortlessly as brilliant Professor X?*

In our own classes, which encompassed three years of coursework from M.A. to doctoral candidacy, we took our share of knocks from tough professors. Some humiliated; some illuminated. You learned—or burned. And everyone smoked—pipes, cigarettes, brown cigarillos—all throughout three-hour-long seminars in window-shut rooms. The workload was not sugarcoated; every graduate seminar (and we took several at a time) required that we read at least one book a week. Often, these books were 400, 500, 600 pages long. *Grundrisse. Women in the Muslim World. Women of the Republic. Mary Chesnut's Civil War. An Economic History of Women in America. Incidents in the Life of a Slave Girl. Women's Life and Work in the Southern Colonies. Population and History. Marriage and Fertility. Surpassing the Love of Men. A Heritage of Her Own. Women in Western Political Thought. Goddesses, Whores, Wives and Slaves. The Glory of Hera.* No one had a computer until 1987 or so; for all the years of our coursework and research, we typed and retyped everything, and kept file cards of notes.

I, who had always been head of the class from pre-kindergarten to college graduation, suddenly had to tread water just to keep up. By the second week of that first semester I was flat on my back with strep throat, literally losing my voice just at the point when I hoped to sound intelligent if called on in class.

In so many ways, large and small, my new classmates and friends, all older, mentored me throughout the notorious process of becoming a doctoral candidate in history. "How's your work coming along?" asked my graduate colleague Bill—the first time any man I knew respectfully referred to the study of women's history as *work*. "Basic teaching advice? Never walk into the classroom without your lecture outline written down," said Tracy. "Look, there are indeed a lot of crazy people here. But you're not one of them," said Deb. "If I could just get four hours of work done a day—four unbroken hours of work," sighed Stephanie. I wanted, too, to work all day and, without somehow becoming crazy, to become like these scholarly women I was befriending. I'd never before been so immersed in a workplace of dynamically intellectual women, all of whom intimidated, inspired, or challenged me in turn. At last I was in an environment where an obsession with documenting women's lives was accepted as the normal career choice for a grown-up. It was heaven—and hell.

But with the exception of one required class, Teaching College History, which everyone complained about having to take, we received little training in what I'd now consider the basics: plotting undergraduate courses, confronting plagiarism in term papers, managing students who seemed mentally unstable or appeared to be in an abusive relationship.

Since the passage of the Americans with Disabilities Act in 1992, it's now standard practice for college students with special needs to get support from a campus disabilities office. Diagnoses ranging from post-traumatic stress to ADHD to depression and dyslexia need not be barriers to outstanding classroom work, and today faculty are alerted ahead of time when students have conditions affecting academic performance. But how history faculty should negotiate with students in crisis, or how to adapt a syllabus to different learning abilities, was never addressed in our preparation for college teaching during the mid-1980s.

We had perhaps one exercise in putting together a syllabus, and two chances to give a sample lecture with doctoral peers and teachers offering feedback. That was it. To be sure, there were mentors like Professor Charles Forcey who pushed exacting standards of scholarly format, testing us all on the writing standards we could then pass on to our own undergraduate students. But the general outlook, in the history department, was that good teaching played second fiddle to good research, and that enthusiastic teachers were sometimes failed scholars. Although I received very appreciative feedback from students about my work as their teaching assistant, those reviews did not matter much in faculty assessments of my potential. While I liked my professors and they often liked me, I found some of their own behaviors distasteful. A few notorious tenured faculty showed up drunk, fell asleep during their own seminars, or made sweeping homophobic pronouncements in class, and at least one visiting scholar sexually harassed female grad students. This was not the kind of professor I was determined to become. There were definite values I'd internalized long ago at Carolina Friends School:

> Students are paying tuition for an education; they should never be insulted or shamed by their instructors, especially during class. Students should not be made to feel "dumb" for asking a question—too many young women, in particular, already preface their comments in class with "Um, like, this is probably really stupid, but . . ."
>
> The teacher needs to be accessible, not just available: Eccentric or intimidating behaviors inhibit learning. Students should not be afraid to visit office hours.
>
> Acknowledging a student's effort can coexist with more critical feedback. When grading, it's no crime to begin with encouragement: *Your second page is strong, clear, well-documented.* Then push for improvement: *Page one needs work.* What's not helpful is a withering declaration such as "Well, this is certainly very bad," the only comment offered by one of my first dissertation readers.

Since I had already made up my mind that I would be teaching U.S. women's history, I assumed I might serve as a teaching assistant for the women's studies program, thereby gaining important experience with student responses to academic feminism. But at Binghamton, at that time, there was a tall Berlin Wall between *women's history* and *women's studies*. They were separate disciplines, with separate funding, and only the history department offered a doctorate as well as M.A. and B.A. degrees. This lack of cooperation seemed, to me, a waste as well as a deception: The women's history and women's studies students attended all the same rallies, cared about the same issues, rejoiced in the same films, and regularly took road trips together to Smedley's, the local women's bookstore in Ithaca. But as historians-to-be, my peers and I were supposed to look down on the women's studies faculty. It was a major breakthrough when I lobbied for and actually won the right to be a graduate teaching assistant for the Women in Film course: one precious semester of border-crossing.

This background is important because I learned a great deal about what not to do, and how not to be, as various faculty came and went, warred with each other, behaved inappropriately with graduate students entrusted to them, and otherwise offered negative role modeling—just as many professors also impressed, uplifted, enlightened, and truly mentored us. And, contrary to what many people think goes on in women's history training, we had no secret indoctrination in radical feminism. Nor was there any secret handbook on how to indoctrinate our own students or "turn them gay" (at least, I'm still waiting for my copy). If anything, there was a tendency toward restraint on the history of sexuality: In the early 1980s there was *no* coursework on gay and lesbian history, which today would be an unacceptable curricular over-sight. While I had many lesbian classmates, none considered the possibility of a doctoral dissertation on lesbian history; graduate student Rochella Thorpe was the first to step boldly in this direction in 1989. Our private lives were separate from our academic work; indeed, I undertook a study of Hasidic Judaism as my Ph.D. project. Like graduate students everywhere, we read our brains out, graded numberless blue books, attended conferences, took notes, and prepared with dread and panic for the day of our Ph.D. orals or dissertation defenses. I took my oral exams on my twenty-fifth birthday. Three years later, ten minutes after successfully defending my doctoral dissertation, I left my dress suit in the history department bathroom, changed into hiking clothes, and as the newly minted Dr. Morris I ascended the nature preserve trail behind our campus and stood on the hilltop, yelling, *Yes.*

How does one put together a women's studies class? The first one I ever taught was Women and Work. It was easy to assemble with the input from a department bursting with labor historians, and 1986 was a year when the debate over women in full-time vs. part-time job slots was the subject of a much-publicized trial, *Sears v. EEOC* (women's history professors were brought in as expert witnesses for both sides). Binghamton selected a few teaching assistants every term to teach adult continuing-ed courses, so I was teaching college almost full-time at age 24, although paid roughly $560 a month to do so. By age 26, I had a good four syllabi in my portfolio, and had graded (as a

T.A. and in my own courses) more than one thousand undergraduate papers, though I would not enter the academic market for a "real" job until I was 27.

The absurd hype surrounding women's studies—*What goes on in those classes? Do y'all just give each other gynecological exams?*—can be deflated with a few sample syllabi. Once and for all, the truth: In this field, as in any other, students read books, take tests, write papers, sit in chairs. At the end of this chapter are two sample syllabi from courses I have taught since 1996: Women in Western Civilization and Women and War.

What's Changed since I Started Teaching?

The one-woman show I wrote primarily drew from experiences between 1974 and 1993, an important era for "mainstreaming" women's studies. The field has continued to attract controversy, but now it's an accepted and popular choice for students satisfying electives in the humanities or social sciences. Some enroll out of sheer curiosity, or because (as they tell me) they seek relief from courses where women are not mentioned once in the syllabus. But the biggest problem for women's studies faculty on campus today is not, in fact, organized backlash to a feminist curriculum. More often, it's the increasingly ugly and competitive confrontations over grades.

Much to our chagrin, women's studies has succeeded in becoming just like any other class—except that young women are probably worse than young men at keeping their cool after getting a low grade. Guys who get a B on their midterm merely shrug and go out for pizza. Young women cry, complain, and confront. Office hours have turned out to be very different from what I expected, particularly as I've logged time as faculty at some very competitive universities: Harvard, Georgetown, George Washington. Here, the burning question bringing students to my door is not *When will women have equal rights and opportunities in every land?* It's *What could I possibly have done to deserve this A–?* And this is as good an indication as any of the priorities we're seeing on campus. The focus, alas, has shifted from activism to self-interest.

For the present generation of college women, the quest for perfectionism magnifies a grade of A– into a personal slight, a career-ending debacle, a punitive abyss of failure. After being hand-held and tutored into high test scores, many students arrive at college feeling entitled to top grades forevermore. Anything less than an A+ signifies "loser," a world-shattering diss, banishment from the educational equivalent of upper-middle-class standing. Thus, for the past decade or more, the vindictive e-mail I receive is almost never from a student objecting, say, to studies in feminist history. No; instead, my hate mail comes from female students who earn less than a straight A on any assignment.

No matter how clearly I explain the breakdown of graded assignments, or my policy of assisting with rough drafts, those students who are not quite writing at college level—or who plagiarize, wittingly or not, from lightweight websites—storm the gates of my office in outrage within seconds of receiving that first B–. The stress meltdown, once a student realizes she never quite learned to cite sources correctly, leads to denial. Then acrimony. Then bargaining. It's a progression not unlike the classic grief stages explained in Elisabeth Kubler-Ross's *On Death and Dying.* And it's young women cultivated toward unhealthy perfectionism who react the worst, who fall apart, crying and threatening. Few take suggestions for improvement seriously, instead responding with counterattack or self-hatred.

Much has been written about the entitlement attitude, and parents' roles in fostering it. Consider these recent books: Alan Eisenstock's *The Kindergarten Wars: The Battle to Get into America's Best Private Schools;* Alyssa Quart's *Hothouse Kids: The Dilemma of the Gifted Child;* Madeline Levine's *The Price of Privilege: How Parental Pressure and Material Advantage Are Creating a Generation of Disconnected and Unhappy Kids;* and Alexandra Robbins's *The Overachievers: The Secret Lives of Driven Kids.* The present generation is both helped and hindered by easy internet access: It's easy to craft a term paper by cutting and pasting from web sources, and even easier to zip off a high-toned e-mail when the professor cites you for plagiarizing. "I know you asked us not to send complaints by e-mail, but this is not a complaint. This is a request for clarification about my grade. You must have made a mistake. How could I end up with a B? I came to class. I participated." Women have indeed learned to be more assertive, to speak up for and defend their worth—that's a great thing, and a necessary skill in the workforce. But confrontations over grades express both insecurity and the inability to handle disappointment—the belief that somehow an error equals failure, and that such a blight on the record of one's learning journey is a personal violation. When I point out that an A must be earned, not negotiated, some of those who finessed high school with ease become tantrum-throwing whiners, incapable of diplomacy. I am now almost, but not quite, as tough as the graduate school professors I learned from myself; anything less does invite interrogation. "According to my calculations, I should have an A," some e-mails begin, neatly attacking my math skills. "Look, I don't mean to be a grade-grubbing type," others say as they walk into my office, a clear indication that they *do* mean to be such a person at our very first meeting.

My job is to graduate women's studies majors and minors who are prepared—academically, ethically, and mentally—to work, write, advocate, agitate, publish, protest, and run for office. And I don't want them writing speeches ripped off from Virginia Woolf or relying on websites crafted by sixth-grade bloggers. I'm the one being asked to write complex letters of recommendation for graduate school, law school, an internship with Hillary Clinton. Since women's studies are indeed under attack, we like our students to be impeccable. And my tightened standards have resulted in cries of protest from students unable to slide by with minimal effort. But how do we best communicate to young feminists, especially those aspiring to public service careers, that slipshod ethics will hinder them? When *New York Times Magazine* ethicist Randy Cohen delivered a speech at Georgetown, a female student asked him, "Look, is it ever okay to plagiarize? Like, supposing you had a death in the family, or just a lot of work due?" At GWU, someone overheard one of my own students declaring, over coffee at Starbucks, "Oh, I've done none of the reading! I'll just get the midterm answers from one of her old tests on file."

It's time for a forum on solutions to these issues in our classrooms. At one faculty meeting, a colleague suggested, "The parents must model this behavior, to ask aggressively for what you think you're owed." "No," said another, "it's the business climate today, and the idea that higher education is a business. Grade evaluations are a transaction. Students see themselves as shareholders." And yet another colleague remarked, "Too many early, unearned rewards spoil the medium-achievers." Or what about this: "Wall Street makes millionaires of entrepreneurs under age 25; why should they respect a professor who earns under $40,000?" Later, a friend who is both a middle-school teacher in an affluent suburb and a mother of three told me, "My kids think No means Negotiate."

When students don't like the grade on their exams, and blast off an e-mail, my first caution to them is always *Stop. Think. Would you speak to a male professor this way?* But the women's studies professor is in a unique bind: Feminist theory and praxis invite disruption of established systems, including interrogation of authority. Academic women's studies, under the umbrella of university bureaucracy, is now part of the Establishment—if not Big Sister, then a strumpet whose annoying rules should be flouted. Authority figures carping about punctuation, footnotes, and what forms of address are proper in student-teacher e-mails do provoke feelings of rebellion. And once feminism turns into a subject you can *do badly in,* it's not about personal and political liberation any more, but about staying atop the dean's list.

Women in Western Civilization

Welcome! This course offers an overview of women's social, legal, and political status in the West: from the onset of civilization up to the "second wave" of feminism in the 1970s. We will examine women's assigned roles in religion, the family, the workplace, and political life, noting the changing nature of *a woman's place* in each period of history. We'll also consider the conflicting expectations for women of different race and class backgrounds. Lectures will be lively and provocative, addressing the readings; discussion sections will ensure extra time for questions and developing written work.

Coursework

You must attend class having completed the readings for each lecture, and you must turn in all written assignments on time—no extensions, no e-mailing or faxing papers from out of town. There will be one in-class midterm exam, one final exam paper, and two short papers. The final grade will be based upon these four assignments plus attendance and participation in sections. Your greatest challenge will be correct citation of scholarly sources: plagiarism is a violation of the University honor code—and my honor code.

Use of Wikipedia, or any other online encyclopedia source, is forbidden for academic work.

Textbooks

Riane Eisler, *The Chalice and the Blade*
The Guerrilla Girls, *Bedside Companion to the History of Western Art*
Helga Harriman, *Women in the Western Heritage*
Gerda Lerner, *The Creation of Feminist Consciousness*
Sarah Pomeroy, *Goddesses, Whores, Wives and Slaves*
Alice Rossi, *The Feminist Papers*
Deborah Grey White, *Ar'n't I a Woman?*
Virginia Woolf, *A Room of One's Own*

Th, Sept. 2: First class. Introduction to the idea of separate spheres; definitions of women's history from Goddess worship to God the Father.

Tu, Sept. 7: Prehistoric images of women in art and spiritual practice. READ: Harriman, intro. & ch. 1; Eisler, ch. 1 & 2.

Th, Sept. 9: The emergence of patriarchy: control of women in the Babylonian Code of Hammurabi. READ: Eisler, ch. 3–5.

Tu, Sept. 14: Women's roles in Egyptian and Hebrew society: queens, pharaohs, temple priestesses, the onset of monotheism. READ: Harriman, ch. 2; Eisler, ch. 6 & 7.

Th, Sept. 16: Continuing discussion of women in Jewish law: commandments, purity, scholarship, divorce, and leadership. Readings from religious commentaries; the different creation stories of man and woman in Genesis, the punishment of Eve.

Tu, Sept. 21: Women in ancient Greece: Goddess imagery, Spartan sacrifice, and civil law. READ: Harriman, ch. 3; Eisler, ch. 8; Pomeroy, pp. 1–148.

Th, Sept. 23: Women's lives in early Rome. READ: Harriman, ch. 3; Pomeroy, pp. 149–230. First short paper assignment handed out today: Address the shift from Goddess worship to language and ritual honoring a male God in monotheism and emerging law.

Tu, Sept. 28: Early Christianity, the fourth-century Church fathers, celibacy, and sex roles. READ: Eisler, ch. 9; Lerner, ch. 3 & 7.

Th, Sept. 30: Women in medieval culture: working lives of queens, serfs, and peasants. READ: Harriman, ch. 5.

Tu, Oct. 5: Scholarly women, religious mystics, and convent communities. READ: Harriman, ch. 6; Lerner, ch. 4. Music composed by Hildegard of Bingen will be played.

Th, Oct. 7: First short paper due in class. No readings today; film, *The Burning Times,* examining the legacy of European witch trials.

Tu, Oct. 12: Women artists and the Renaissance. READ: Harriman, ch. 7, and all of the Guerrilla Girls textbook. Field trip to the National Museum of Women in the Arts.

Th, Oct. 14: Women in the Protestant Reformation and the Early Modern period. READ: Harriman, ch. 8, and Eisler, ch. 10 & 11.

Th, Oct. 21: From pre-industrial agrarian life to the economy of the industrial revolution: families going "out" to work. No readings: review for midterm exam.

Tu, Oct. 26: Midterm exam

Th, Oct. 28: The slave trade: abolitionists, slave-owning women, and the legal status of female slaves in America. READ: all of White, and Rossi, pp. 241–322.

Tu, Nov. 2: Election Day: Please vote! Republican motherhood in the 19th century. READ: Lerner, ch. 6 & 9; Rossi, pp. 1–143. Midterms returned; second short paper assignment handed out: Discuss the arguments for and against female education in any time period up to World War I.

Th, Nov. 4: The first wave of American feminism, from Christian reformers to the Seneca Falls convention. READ: Harriman, ch. 10; Lerner, ch. 10;

and Rossi, essays by John Stuart Mill, Elizabeth Cady Stanton, and Susan B. Anthony.

Tu, Nov. 9: The emergence of women's colleges, public schools, and teaching as a female profession. READ: Lerner, ch. 1, 2, & 8, and all of Woolf.

Th, Nov. 11: The suffrage movement in America: actions, documents, and organizations. READ: Rossi, pp. 407–470.

Tu, Nov. 16: Women's roles in World War I and the Russian Revolution. READ: Harriman, ch. 11; Rossi, all of part 3.

Th, Nov. 18: Immigration at the turn of the century; Irish, Italian, and Jewish women workers in American factories, mills, and homes. Second short paper due.

Tu, Nov. 23: A brief history of birth control from the Comstock Laws to Margaret Sanger and the eugenics movement of the 1920s. READ: Rossi, section on Sanger.

Th, Nov. 25: No class—Thanksgiving Day

Tu, Nov. 30: World War II: working women and WACS; the internment of Japanese American women and children; women in the Holocaust as Nazis and resistance fighters. READ: Eisler, ch. 12.

Th, Dec. 2: The Cold War and the climate for women in the 1950s—from McCarthyism to Simone de Beauvoir—and the second wave of feminism in the 1960s and '70s, culminating in Title IX law, *Roe v. Wade,* and the failure of the equal rights amendment. READ: Harriman, ch. 12; Rossi, Beauvoir chapter; and Lerner, ch. 11.

Final exam paper due one week from today.

Women and War

Welcome! This course examines the impact of war and militarism on women's lives, with an emphasis on U.S. history. Topics will include women's roles as soldiers, as wives and mothers of servicemen, industrial war workers, revolutionaries and guerrillas, spies and traitors, heroines and martyrs, prostitutes and "comfort women." You will be asked to critique the functions assigned to women in wartime, and to analyze different concepts of female patriotism. We'll also debate current issues concerning women in combat, the ban on lesbian and gay soldiers, rape as a war crime, women and torture, and media coverage of women involved in peace activism and security work.

Coursework

You must arrive in class on time and prepared to discuss the readings assigned for the day. Written work includes a four-page reaction paper to news coverage of war; a midterm exam in class; and a final paper due on our last day of class. Grades are based on these three assignments plus attendance, and will be weighted toward your best work. Consistent lateness, overdue work, plagiarism, and other evils are not acceptable. Please be respectful of your classmates' viewpoints, as we will discuss controversial and even painful material; a mature attitude is essential.

Textbooks

Ayala Emmett, *Our Sisters' Promised Land*
Cynthia Enloe, *Maneuvers*
Leisa Meyer, *Creating G.I. Jane*
Mine Okubo, *Citizen 13660*
Marjane Satrapi, *Persepolis*
Margaret Stetz and Bonnie Oh, *Legacies of the Comfort Women*
Matthew Stibbe, *Women in the Third Reich*
Philippa Strum, *Women in the Barracks*

Additional Books on Reserve

John Armor and Peter Wright, *Manzanar*
Margaret Higonnet, ed., *Lines of Fire*
Chiura Obata, *Topaz Moon*
Alice Rossi, ed., *The Feminist Papers*
Zainab Salbi, *The Other Side of War*
Michael O. Tunnell and George W. Chilcoat, *The Children of Topaz*
Keith Walker, *A Piece of My Heart*
Nancy Baker Wise and Christy Wise, *A Mouthful of Rivets*
C. Vann Woodward, ed., *Mary Chesnut's Civil War*

Articles

Jerry Cadick, "On Being a Warrior," *Newsweek* (Apr. 14, 1997): 16
Dan Eggen, "Permissible Assaults Cited in Graphic Detail," *Washington Post* (Apr. 6, 2008): A03
Melissa S. Embser-Herbert, "When Women Abuse Power, Too," *Washington Post* (May 16, 2004): B01
Meghan Gibbons, "On the Home Front," *Washington Post* (Oct. 16, 2005): B03
Kristin Henderson, "A Woman's Touch," *Washington Post Magazine* (Feb. 24, 2008): 16

Anne Hull and Dana Priest, "A Wife's Battle," *Washington Post* (Oct. 14, 2007): A01

Michelle Malkin, "Candidates Ignore 'Security Moms' at Their Peril," *USA Today* (July 20, 2004)

James Webb, "Women Can't Fight," *The Washingtonian* (Nov. 1979): 144

Tu, Jan. 16: First class: introduction. Discussion of course requirements, and an overview of current issues and stereotypes: women warriors, queens, pirates, strategists, crusaders, captives, Amazons.

Th, Jan. 18: Are women suited for military life? What accommodations have been made in the past generation for women training in formerly "male" military command roles? READ: *Maneuvers,* preface and ch. 1; James Webb, "Women Can't Fight."

Tu, Jan. 23: Women as future citizens: issues of the American Revolution. READ: *Maneuvers,* ch. 2, and letters of Abigail Adams to John Adams, spring 1776, in *The Feminist Papers.*

Th, Jan. 25: Legacies of distrust, widowhood, and chivalry: black and white women in the American Civil War. READ: excerpts from *Mary Chesnut's Civil War.*

Tu, Jan. 30: Empire-building and race: from the defeat of Hawaii's queen to policies of Teddy Roosevelt. READ: *Maneuvers,* ch. 3.

Th, Feb. 1: World War I: causes, mothers' resistance, and feminist pacifism. READ: Emmeline Pankhurst, "Votes for Women"; Lida Heymann, "An Appeal to Women"; and Jane Addams, "Women and Internationalism," in *Lines of Fire.*

Tu, Feb. 6: World War I: women's participation as patriots, ambulance drivers, laborers, and suffragist protests. READ: Bessie Beatty, "The Battalion of Death"; Maria Botchkareva, "No Man's Land"; and Katherine North, "A Driver at the Front," in *Lines of Fire.*

Th, Feb. 8: World War I: the Russian Revolution and its impact on foreign policy and feminism. READ: Alexandra Kollontai, "Who Needs the War?" in *Lines of Fire.*

Tu, Feb. 13: World War II: the formation of women's military units. READ: *Creating G.I. Jane,* prologue through ch. 6.

Th, Feb. 15: First paper due. Film in class: *The Life and Times of Rosie the Riveter.* READ: excerpts from Wise and Wise, *A Mouthful of Rivets.*

Tu, Feb. 20: World War II: theories and policies of Nazi Germany with regard to women's roles in motherhood, marriage, the workplace, and national ideology. READ: chapter excerpts from *Women in the Third Reich*.

Th, Feb. 22: World War II: the internment of Japanese Americans. READ: *Citizen 13660*, and, on reserve: *Topaz Moon; Manzanar; The Children of Topaz*.

Tu, Feb. 27: The postwar atomic age, the Cold War, and anxiety over nuclear weapons. Film in class: *Atomic Cafe*.

Th, Mar. 1: Vietnam and the antiwar counterculture of the 1960s; gender roles for mothers and girlfriends. READ: *Maneuvers*, ch. 6, and *A Piece of My Heart*, on reserve.

Tu, Mar. 6: Midterm exam

Th, Mar. 8: International Women's Day. Film on Vietnamese and American women war widows: *Regret to Inform*.

Mar. 12–16: No class—Spring Break

Tu, Mar. 20: Wives, families, motherhood and childcare issues in military life. READ: *Maneuvers*, ch. 4, 5, & 7.

Th, Mar. 22: "Comfort women" and the legacy of wartime sexual slavery, including tactics of ethnic rape in Serbia and Sudan. READ: *Legacies of the Comfort Women*.

Tu, Mar. 27: Changing roles for women in the U.S. military academies and leadership positions. READ: *Women in the Barracks*.

Th, Mar. 29: No class—Easter/Passover holidays

Tu, Apr. 3: Lesbians in the military and the official "Don't Ask, Don't Tell" ban. READ: *Creating G.I. Jane*, ch. 7. Guest speaker from the Servicemembers Legal Defense Fund.

Th, Apr. 5: Religious warfare and conflict over the creation of modern-day Israel. READ: *Our Sisters' Promised Land*, ch. 1–3.

Tu, Apr. 10: Continuing discussion of women's roles in the Israeli-Palestinian conflict. READ: *Our Sisters' Promised Land*, ch. 4–6.

Th, Apr. 12: War and Islamic revolution through a child's eyes: the graphic novel *Persepolis*. See the film *Persepolis*, now playing in theatres.

Tu, Apr. 17: Terrorism, 9/11, and the American response. Who are the new female terrorist suspects—and the so-called "security moms"? How have changing security measures altered women's lives?

Th, Apr. 19: Women and the war in Iraq. READ: "On the Home Front."

Tu, Apr. 24: Torture and diplomacy: Are women truly less violent, or uniquely suited to peacemaking? What were U.S. responses to implications of servicewomen in the Abu Ghraib torture scandals? READ: "When Women Abuse Power, Too."

Th, Apr. 26: A look at Women for Women International and other aid groups. Is there a new gendered activism countering wartime abuses of women and girls in Sudan, Rwanda, and Afghanistan? READ: Zainab Salbi, *The Other Side of War,* on reserve.

Tu, May 1: Last class. Your final paper is due today; be prepared to present an abstract of your research in class. Papers will be graded and returned to you by next Monday, May 7.

4.

Scene Four, 1987
Can I Talk to You in Private?

Professor Morris?

I'm real sorry to bother you like this, but could we talk privately for a moment?

You see . . . I really enjoy your women's studies class. I do, I love it. And I want to finish out the semester. But my husband . . . he feels differently. He thinks it's a lot of radical ideas and he wants me to drop your class right now. He just doesn't like me going out at night to take a women's studies class, even though it's just once a week and I told him over and over it does count toward me finishing my business degree.

Professor . . . I think it would help me out if you could just come have supper with us and meet my husband. He'd see that you're a fine, smart person and I would so appreciate your reaching out to him! He's not a bad guy—he just doesn't understand why all of a sudden I'm reading these women's lib books. I guess he's worried you might try to corrupt me or something. He's real traditional.

You would come to dinner? Oh, thank you! Thank you so much! I'll make something special—and it would be an honor to have you in our home. Just don't pay any mind to what my husband might say to you. Just between us, he comes from kind of a small-minded family.

OPPOSITE PAGE: Performing *Revenge* on-stage at the D.C. Pride Festival, 1995

What could I say? Yes, of course I went to have dinner with my adult student and her family. At 36, she was twelve years older than me, raising three boys, working part-time in real estate, and now going back to college for a business major. I wanted her in my class. And so I went to meet her husband and win his approval. I talked lightly about camping and hiking and movies while he stared at my bust over the spiced ham. Finally, at the end of the meal, he stood up to shake my hand, saying, "Well, little lady! I confess I thought you'd have horns on your head and come dressed in a suit of armor carrying a battleax. But I reckon you're woman enough after all." His wife, my student, drove me home in silence. She later earned an A.

This is a difficult scene to re-enact onstage. It's the only one in which I become another individual, whose true identity I've carefully masked with certain changes. Remembering that day, that interaction, I close my eyes in preparation of becoming—for an audience—a student I once taught. I imagine the enormous courage it took for her to enroll in my class, to defy her angry husband, and to approach me during office hours, inviting me to supper. I was 24 to her 36, and must have seemed so young to her. Young enough to please her husband's eye.

For faculty who work with returning adult students, or at campuses with a substantial commuter population of older, married undergraduates, certain issues do become familiar: A student misses an important class because she can't find a babysitter. Or her child is sick, and she misses many classes. Family issues overlap with school time, and a sympathetic professor has to be flexible. I was very, very lucky to be hired, just after earning my M.A., to teach night courses on women's history under the terms of my graduate assistantship. But I was unprepared for husbands who thought me a bad influence on their wives.

"No more school," snarls the husband in *The Burning Bed,* one of television's first widely broadcast movies about domestic violence (adapted from the book of the same title). Jealousy and suspicion toward wives and mothers who go back to school, even for basic literacy instruction, are problems in many developing nations, as shown in the documentary *Hope Is a Literate Woman.* It doesn't matter if the goal is self-improvement for the betterment of the community, or a family-centered desire to learn to read to one's children; "good" women don't go out at night—especially unchaperoned by men. Bengali physician, literacy activist, and author Taslima Nasrin was threatened with murder (placed under Muslim *fatwa*) for teaching women to read; most of us know about the ongoing struggle for female education in Afghanistan, where the violent Taliban militias closed all schools for girls during the 1990s.[1] Although many Americans concerned themselves with Taliban strategy in Afghanistan only after September 11, 2001, groups like Eleanor Smeal's Feminist Majority Foundation had been reporting on the girls' schooling crisis since 1994. In 1995, outraged that Taliban warlords had shut down education for women in an entire country, I had letters tattooed on my writing arm so that every day, for the rest of my life, I'd remember how privileged I am to be a literate woman. (In fair weather, my exposed tattoo is great for sparking discussions about female education.)

By day, most women carry a double burden of employment and childcare or housework, so night school is often their only option. Pressure from male family elders can quickly dash women's hopes of education. I was sorry to find this phenomenon alive and well in America.

"My boyfriend and I had a fight about this class," many undergraduates begin agitatedly. "He says it's turning me into a . . ." And I look quickly to make sure this student bears no bruises, ensuring she means "a fight" in the sense of verbal argument. Sometimes it's the quiet ones, the ones who disappear, who live with conflict. Like Emma (not her real name).

Emma was a brilliant student of mine in the early 1990s, when I taught at a university near a large and isolated army base. A number of students had boyfriends at the base or, in Emma's case, an abusive relationship. I had no inkling about Emma's private life and knew her only as a responsible, hard-working, and creative student who suddenly stopped turning in work and racked up one absence after another. When I confronted her with an academic warning, she explained her situation in painful detail: She was being stalked and harassed by her ex-boyfriend. Terrified to leave her room, she could not escape his intrusion, which escalated through hate mail and calls. Apparently, she had had an abortion, and afterward he sent letter after letter to her with "Happy Birthday" cards and other macabre notes, purportedly from the baby they never had.

---

1. See the interview with Taslima Nasrin and additional chapters on both Taliban and Western religious suppression of female education in *Nothing Sacred: Women Respond to Religious Fundamentalism and Terror,* ed. Betsy Reed (New York: Thunder's Mouth/Nation Books, 2002).

I asked Emma if she had spoken with our campus security officers. She had, and the university knew about the obscene letters, which arrived regularly. But the response, both from campus security and the town police force, was that until her ex-boyfriend actually harmed her physically on campus, there was nothing they could do. I never saw Emma again.

This became a familiar story in my teaching career. At a different campus, a star student was stalked by a Peeping Tom and, unable to sleep nights in fear of his appearance at her window, she failed to turn in an important paper. I was shocked to learn that campus police had advised her to "catch him in the act" by deliberately remaining alone in her room as bait, with a video camera—a situation that seemed very dangerous to me. Another student phoned me during office hours and in a small voice explained that she'd missed her midterm because, she suspected, her drink had been drugged at a party the previous night; she was undergoing tests in the health center.

How does a professor cope with abuse of women as a reality intruding into the women's studies classroom? It's a formidable challenge. For one thing, it has become popular to lament "victim feminism"; since the 1980s, writers ranging from Camille Paglia to Katie Roiphe to Christina Hoff Sommers have questioned the credibility of reports on date rape violence, or the efficacy of campus guidelines meant to curtail sexual assault against women. Following this trend, one year a conservative undergraduate group at Georgetown distributed handbooks to all new female students, directing them to avoid the campus Women's Center due to its advisory programs on college date rape. When I have cited the FBI's own statistics in class, estimating that one in three women are likely to experience rape or sexual assault, often at the hands of an acquaintance or family friend, students object: "I don't know three women who have been raped, so you must be lying." A business professor present at one of my lectures told me I'd never "sell my product" (women's history) by exaggerating and falsifying statistics. A female student suggested loudly that I must have had a "bad experience with men," myself. The topic makes everyone uncomfortable.

No matter how we wish to align statistics in support of our arguments, faculty and students need to be aware that in any college classroom there are women (and men) who have experienced violence and molestation. Would that it were not so! In my own college days, I was privileged to take a popular women's health class at American University, enrolling along with several close friends. In that class of more than sixty students from all backgrounds, we talked about women at high risk for domestic violence, and the factors that made it difficult for battered wives to leave abusive marriages. One day, a student declared, "Well, I don't see why any smart woman would stay in such a situation: She can always leave." To the immediate right of this speaker was an older adult student, who rose from her seat and sobbed, "No, you wouldn't understand what it's like, would you?" "Oh, shit," murmured everyone, as the real world entered the classroom that day. In the quibbling about statistical reporting, it's easy to forget that just one individual's suffering is an outrage. How many women never speak up?

Over the years, I've known quite a few students who missed class due to injuries or court dates related to sexual assault. Some communicated with me through class journal assignments, expressing frustration with a campus justice system they believed favored male athletes. In my sports history class, a male student turned in a paper with the opening line, "Baseball season begins! I'm so happy—baseball represents everything that is good about this country." But the very next paper was a female student's account of being sexually assaulted by a baseball player. Another student in that class had not only been raped by an athlete, but discovered that a video of the incident was being passed around the dorms. She felt there was no way she, a lonely newcomer, would ever be believed in a legal proceeding against one of the most popular males on campus; she had no intention of bringing charges, and simply wanted me to know why she had missed weeks of class.

In this way, women's studies faculty are made aware of events that never make it into the judicial system. The challenge is retaining a boundary between classroom discussion and these students' extra needs; the professor is not a therapist. But in, say, an all-female class of thirty or so, there's a good chance at least half a dozen students may have had some experience with assault. How can an academic discussion on violence against women proceed without becoming uncomfortably personal? When women's studies faculty pause to consider a sensitive application of controversial topics, too often we're charged with teaching "touchy-feely" subject matter.

For some students, having a safe space to re-examine an incident that felt inappropriate may be the first step in taking action, or, at least, framing the situation as part of a pattern in society.

My best friend was attacked right on the quad last fall. Thank God, she was able to get away. This fear of rape is maddening, constant; the administration tries to keep it quiet, but rape and assault occur here all the time.

I work in a sports bar where the police eat and drink at a huge discount. Things happen all the time there—it's an atmosphere of unchecked hegemonic masculinity, a place for men to "be men." But I never felt the need to speak up about anything until last night. I was bringing drinks to one policeman when he said, "What do 10,000 abused women have in common?" The answer: "They don't know how to fucking listen." Wow. The guys started laughing and the bartender thought it was so funny he retold it a couple of times. I guess the policeman saw the look on my face—so he goes, "What? Are you offended or something?" It's just incredible to me that he felt so comfortable talking like that in public. The scary thing is: This is the group of men I'm supposed to call if my partner abuses me.

I play women's club rugby, and rugby songs are vulgar—not just un-p.c. but downright dirty. We had a run-in about this male rugby song, "The S & M Man," which is even mentioned in our class textbook. A male player sang about taking a female rugger and "fucking her until the bitch swears she's straight," or taking a feminist and "fucking her up the ass until she knows her place is in the kitchen." The next verse he started was about "taking a black girl," and at that point one woman threw her beer in his face. We'd been standing there, getting angry and offended, and she was the only one with enough courage to take a stand. It felt like an attack on all twenty-five female athletes in the room.

In a magazine I noticed how terribly skinny the models were, anorexic-looking, and I asked my boyfriend if he thought these women were sexy. He said, "Yes." I said, "But it looks like a guy could break her," and he said, "That's the attraction, honey."

In the gym two days ago a guy was teaching his girlfriend how to do bicep curls. Yet instead of helping her, he grew nasty and frustrated. He flicked her arm hard where her fat jiggled and said, "This is what I want to get rid of." It was public humiliation—she cried. I thought it looked like an abusive relationship. They both knew I was watching.

I attended another college before transferring here and let me tell you, the hockey players at that school were treated like gods—the disrespect they showed women was unbelievable. They referred to their female fans as "puck fucks."

In some instances, disrespect expressed in a sexually aggressive manner can be communicated with a t-shirt slogan. As Cynthia Enloe, Saundra Pollock Stuyvesant, and Brenda Stoltzfus have described in their research on Southeast Asian sex workers' camptowns near U.S. military bases in South Korea and the Philippines, popular souvenirs for American servicemen include a notorious t-shirt announcing: "I may not go down in history but I will go down on your little sister." This novelty shirt surfaced on a young man in the computer lab at George Washington University, where I was printing out a midterm; seated at the computer station next to him was a completely veiled Muslim student from Indonesia. How did his choice of free speech make her feel as she completed her own term paper?

In other cases, male violence has indirectly caused a student to drop out of (or fall behind in) one of my classes. An incident illustrating the intersection of race, class, and gender occurred at one overwhelmingly white university where I taught women's history. My one black student, a very responsible scholar, came to my office in tears because she could not afford the textbooks for my class. Along with each of the students in her residence hall, she had received a bill for damages after some drunken male hallmates destroyed physical property and necessitated a major cleanup job. This was a common policy: the sharing of fines when those responsible for dorm damage did not come forward to accept responsibility. All students living in the affected residence hall were forced to bear a percentage of the damage costs—carpet cleaning, glass replacement, and so on. For the affluent majority, these accumulated "hall fines" appeared as just one more item on a sheet of expenses billed to parents. In the case of my student, however—attending college on a scholarship, and the only woman of color on her hall—the "equal" distribution of fines represented a very real expense of hundreds of dollars not covered by her financial aid. Moreover, she had been informed by the university bursar that if she did not pay the fines promptly, she would be prevented from registering for spring courses and from graduating in the spring. Because she had played no part in the alcohol-fueled party melee, she was mortified to discover that her immigrant parents—school janitors themselves—were actually being billed for others' negligence.

Investigating further, I found that the staff at this university's physical plant were adamant about the fining system, unfair though it might be. The hardworking dorm cleaners were mostly older women from the low-income rural community, more than weary of cleaning up rich students' garbage from food fights and beer binges. Because few students were willing to identify guilty parties after big rampages, fines continued to be forced on entire halls.

According to one academic dean I consulted, the "innocent" were supposed to exert peer pressure so that the more destructive parties would come forward and confess. However, when one of my students did reproach a male friend with an alcohol problem as he began to make a disturbance one night, his response was to hit her in the face. Although he had to leave the college briefly, he returned the following semester, whereas my student withdrew. The message to other students was loud and clear: Intervene with a violent hallmate and you'll get hurt. It's not worth it. Just pay the damn fines.

In these ways and others, the problem of living with and pacifying violent men (or men merely hostile to feminists) preoccupies women's studies students who could otherwise focus on coursework. Faculty are sometimes entrusted with the details, but too often we become aware of a simmering situation only long after a student's academic performance has been compromised by intimidation or abuse. I started my journey into greater understanding of this dynamic back in 1986, more than twenty years ago, with the mildest sort of problem: a fearful married student having to quit class because her husband disapproved of women's studies.

June 29, 2000

Bonnie J. Morris, Ph.D.
Women's Studies Department
George Washington University
2201 G St., N.W.
Washington, D.C. 20052

Dear Dr. Morris:

I am writing to invite you to visit Gallaudet University in the Fall of 2000.

There is considerable interest on our campus in women's issues, and we would love to be able to include you in a series of distinguished speakers. The topics you have written about are so fascinating and diverse that I am sure you would be inspiring to our students. They would be happy to hear about your research experiences and opinions, or to see the "Revenge of the Women's Studies Professor" if that would be appropriate for an undergraduate audience. The Library would develop co-sponsorship with campus groups such as the Honors English and Communication Arts classes to ensure a well-prepared audience.

As I am sure you know, Gallaudet is the only liberal arts university for deaf students in the world, and addressing a deaf audience might be a new and interesting experience for you. Of course we would provide sign language interpreters.

We would also probably be able to provide a modest honorarium.

Invitation to perform at Gallaudet University
with sign language interpretation

5.

Scene Five, 1989
Do We Have to Have So Much Women's History?

Hi, Ralph! Have a seat. Thanks for coming by my office hours. I'll be with you in just a minute.

Okay. You wrote a little note on the bottom of your midterm asking to meet with me—something about being unhappy with the test questions. Your grades are fine; what's on your mind? Are you enjoying U.S. History?

Ah. You think I'm including "too much" women's history. And "all" I ever talk about in class is women's history? You think that due to my bias, you're not getting the "real" education you signed up for. Well, let's see. Do you have your syllabus with you? It shows here that we meet, as a class, thirty times this fall semester. And a total of three of our class lectures focus on women's contributions to America: women in the American Revolution, women who went west as schoolteachers on the frontier, women war workers in the Rosie the Riveter campaign of World War II. That's, hmmm . . . 10 percent of our time studying 52 percent of the American people. Just three talks on women out of thirty.

I knew when I designed this course that looking at gender would be a new approach for most first-year students, so I took care to include a special lecture on the role of fatherhood and male identity in American history. But according to my grade book, you skipped that class. You said you had a fraternity event that day.

So, Ralph, what's really going on here? Hmmm . . . You

say your mother was a feminist and I remind you of her and
her weird friends? Ouch. I'm afraid that's between you and your
family. But let me tell you what my role is as your professor.

I'm here to challenge you in college, and that means you'll get
new books and ideas you were probably not exposed to in high
school. And whenever a person is introduced to new material, it
crowds out the old material for a while; it seems to take up more
space. I'm betting that's why only three talks on women feels like
"all" we ever do is study women in my class. In truth, during the
other twenty-seven classes, "all" we study is men's history. But
that's familiar, and seems more real . . . or valuable . . . or true.
What's more, most women don't feel like they have a right to
complain about getting a one-sided education. Women's history
is a political agenda . . . men's history is "timeless truth." Right?

Maybe I'm the first woman professor you've ever had,
and maybe you've heard from the media or other sources
that women are supposed to be more emotional, less logical,
less intellectual than men. Maybe you feel I'm presenting
one-sided lectures informed by personal emotion, not
research, because I'm a woman. Maybe your mother's
activism has led you to feel that all feminists are "angry."

But, Ralph—it looks like you're the one who's emotional and
angry, about having to sit through three classes on women's lives.

This, again, is a true story. My first job after finishing graduate school
was at California State University–Chico, where I taught 8 AM U.S. history
survey courses to lecture halls packed with first-year students. My department chair, Dale Steiner, had recruited me to incorporate ethnic and women's
history into the curriculum—his own field was immigration history, and we
both lectured on the legacy of working mothers who filled American factories
and sweatshops soon after arriving on Ellis Island. Dale, however, did not get
complaints that he taught "too much" women's history. I did.

My classes included equal numbers of male and female students. Some
had left behind gang affiliation in Los Angeles for a fresh start in college up
north. Others were refugees: Chico had a large Hmong community, and I tutored one gifted young man who had spent his youth in a South Asian refugee
camp little better than a prison. I had adult students completing their teaching
certificates, who worked with me via distance learning; one was a mountain

man who begged me to help treat his children for lice; another abused his distance-learning privileges by phoning me at home and asking for a date. I had one history section for special-needs and probational students, with a trained teaching assistant. That class worked very hard and did well (a different section enrolling more affluent, carefree students chose to cheat on the midterm). And so I was surrounded, daily, by young people who could and did come to me for help. I was highly visible at Chico as one of the few professors active in an antiracism council, where I lent my support to Native American and Palestinian student leaders on campus. My days were filled with the task of mentoring at-risk young men.

It was a more privileged male student who expressed outrage that a general history course required of all first-year students would actually include material on women in America. I was both amused and offended by the way Ralph (not his real name) confronted me in my office. It would not be the first time a student charged that women's history was not "real" history, and over time I grew more adept at handling such encounters, though not without an inward sigh.

How do male students feel, in general, about women's studies? About the subject of women's history? The answer is that there is no generalization, nor should there be, just as I caution my own students against generalizing about "all women" in their research and writing.

Some male students new to women's history, like Ralph, initially feel challenged, left out, even, perhaps, educationally ripped off. It's a big serving of what psychologists call "cognitive dissonance": all of a sudden, after twelve years of American schooling, along comes a class in which famous men aren't the primary focus. But women, too, find changes to the traditional school curriculum discomfiting. And, increasingly, women have joined the ranks of conservative student associations and think tanks, most (if not all) of which criticize women's studies as an unwelcome innovation. By the late 1980s, young women who came of age in the Reagan era could be far harsher critics of academic feminism than their sometimes more liberal male classmates. Throughout my teaching years, I have found that most guys who actually *took a class* left convinced that it was a positive experience and that I was a decent, unbiased teacher. Some became my strongest allies.

I quickly found that personal, face-to-face encounters during office hours were preferable to being attacked in the media by both males and females who had never taken a women's studies course, but enjoyed trashing the field. My entry into academia coincided with a new wave of conservative student newspapers funded by off-campus organizations. The *Dartmouth Review,*

Georgetown Academy, Georgetown Independent, and *Independence Magazine* at George Washington University were four such publications appearing over time at institutions where I held appointments. All took aim at women's history courses as forums for useless or dangerous propaganda. Though supportive of a free press, I was troubled by several incidents in which well-scrubbed young men published editorials lampooning my courses without ever meeting me, visiting my classroom, reading through a syllabus, or otherwise adhering to basic principles of accurate reporting.

On several different occasions, I was tricked into media appearances that had the sole purpose of mocking women's studies (although I was told the program had a different theme, or that I was being selected to give viewers a real look inside a women's history classroom). This began while I was still in graduate school at Binghamton University in 1989. A male classmate, active in conservative causes, who had never spoken to me directly in six years of graduate student life, suddenly approached me in a friendly way and asked if I'd like to represent our women's history Ph.D. program on a campus radio talk show. He flattered me by suggesting I'd be a great speaker on the air, and told me I'd simply be answering questions about the women's history field. I went home and prepared like hell, boning up on the history of women's history, eager to promote our excellent doctoral program. However, when I arrived at the radio station, a technician startled me by smirking, "We expect a great catfight today," and then the program host introduced me to the other guest, explaining, "This is the head of the county Right-to-Life chapter; you'll be debating her on air. Ready? Here we go." Before I could protest that this was *not* the topic I'd been asked to address, the "on air" lights flashed, and my counterpart leaned into the microphone and began the hour by shouting, "Abortion is murder!" Five minutes later, the same graduate student who had set me up phoned in "anonymously" (though I recognized his voice) to comment that the pro-life representative was far more articulate than the unprepared young feminist, and that this showed how badly Binghamton's program trained its future women's history professors.

I was furious, but within three years I fell into a similar trap. In the early 1990s, while interviewing for jobs at the annual meeting of the American Historical Association, I attended a panel on women in the history profession, and after identifying myself as a young women's history specialist I was approached by some filmmakers. They liked me and liked what I had said. Was I interested in representing women's history in a documentary film? Thrilled, I agreed to give them an interview. I later found that their project, *Campus Cultural Wars,* was intended to "expose" political correctness in academia by "re-creating," with actors, controversial moments at U.S. colleges. The program looked unfavorably at feminism in the classroom. When it finally aired, my own smiling face served as background for docudrama segments trashing women's studies. Another program I interviewed for, produced by a woman, resulted in mocking my class. Exploiting audiences' pre-existing stereotypes about the women's studies classroom makes good copy, but does little to educate.

Needless to say, I've learned to proceed cautiously, demanding of potential interviewers, "Are you here to get the real story, or to make fun of my profession?" However, one rarely has total control over a journalist's final product. I've had both male and female students assure me they just wanted "facts" about women's studies, yet somehow I then ended up party to my own vilification in columns published for right-wing student newspapers. Typical slams on my courses in *Independent*-style papers included these lines:

Women's studies has a negative rate of return. How come?
Because it qualifies you for nothing, makes it so you can contribute
nothing, and gives you the opportunity for nothing. . . .

The knowledge, if you can call it that, acquired in
Athletics and Gender does little to make you a productive
student. You might say, "Wow, this crap we make
up as we go along is really interesting. . . ."

It is doubtful that this for-credit course could be more politically
correct and yet utterly ridiculous at the same time.

Throughout the 1990s, media campaigns that sought to discredit women's studies with comments like these scared away both male and female students. But if female students were made to feel that studying their own sex was intellectual foolishness, or a pathetic path to identifying as a victim, male students had an added advisory: Women's studies teaches that men are the enemy. What self-respecting guy would enroll?

The most misunderstood notion of women's history in higher education is that it is simply about male bashing. In truth, what startles both women and men is not an anti-male focus, but exposure to a focus on women's cultural and historical contributions. The fact that, in order to succeed, women frequently had to overcome legal restrictions not imposed on men is an un-avoidable part of the story; but looking at where gender meets power is just as salient as legal history of race, class, or religious identity.

Adjusting to this shift does mean that male students' experiences in women's history courses can differ substantially from those of their female classmates. Some men will feel attacked, angry, and otherwise self-conscious or targeted when confronted with evidence of patriarchal societies' limitations on female power.

This is not too different from the discomfort white students may experience in a seminar on the history of American slavery. "I didn't make those laws." "I'm not responsible for those problems." "I'm not a racist; maybe my grandparents were, but not me!" These are classic responses from members of a majority or privileged group as they immerse in the counterpoint history of the oppressed. Yes, a women's studies professor needs to be aware of how male students respond to course material on institutionalized sexism. But her job is not to play therapist. I had already been involved for many years in Unlearning Racism workshops at different events around the country, and knew how I had felt, initially, as the lone white woman hearing black participants' stories of discrimination. I, too, had that inward shout, "But I'm one of the good guys—I'm here, aren't I?" Men who experience those feelings while taking women's history, who sometimes for the first time ever are a minority in a classroom, have my sympathy. I know that they, like me, are daring to interrogate an American past where all have *not* been equal in the eyes of law and custom.

The real male bashing comes from male students' friends and family members, who can't believe that a normal guy would bother to take a class about women.

My girlfriend laughs at the fact that I have taken two of your classes.

One of my friends feels that there is no reason for a man to take any gender course. He thinks that most people, male or female, who take such a course are gay.

Some people have asked me, "What do you talk about in that women's history course?" They don't think there could be enough information to fill an entire semester!

When I go to your class, friends say, "How is that male-bashing course going?"

One friend's warning to me was, "My roommate
freshman year took a women's studies class, and halfway
through the semester he started wearing clogs."

When I told my friends that I was taking this class, they all
made fun of me, asking why I would want to be in a room
with a bunch of feminists. My friends thought they would
tear me apart. I asked some male friends for the first word
that came to mind when I said "feminist." Here are some
responses: lesbian, bitch, Communist, liberal, Hillary Clinton.

My mom argued with me! I thought she would respect
the fact that I was trying to learn something. She sees this
class as too controversial. My mother has been involved
in charity work for the Junior League all her life, but she
feels that women should not be in the work force.

A male friend said, "Man, how can you deal with those women's
classes? That must be hell." I told him that your classes were
nothing close to what I had expected and that I really enjoyed them
after being so burnt-out of boring history. It blew this guy out of
the water that I was taking two classes in women's history, with a
feminist professor, and that I recommended both classes to him!

My parents are worried about my grades. When I told my
father I was taking women's history, he asked if "that feminist"
was gonna burn me or if I "sucked it up all semester."

I have a friend at the University of Georgia who can't believe my
school lets me get credit for studying about women. He said he
thought it was "gay" that I was taking a girls' class. So I told
him I thought it was "gay" that he was flunking out of school.

I came to college for athletics and joined an athletic fraternity.
Today is the first day I dared mention your class; actually,
I brought up the subject of women in political office. The
reaction I got was, "Lesbian manhaters, that's all they are,"
and then my own sexual preference came into question. I
gave up in frustration. I can't talk about class in my house.

And one honest, thoughtful young man talked about this incident:

This conversation about feminism took place in my fraternity. My brothers were talking about the women's movement and the kind of women involved. I sat there listening to them blast women who identified as feminists. The problem was, one guy's girlfriend is starting to be more active on women's issues and he feels this will be the downfall of their relationship. She spoke of women's lack of political representation. He refuted by speaking of tradition and men and women's proper roles in society. As the conversation went on my brother got more annoyed and argumentative. He is known for his short fuse and his outbursts. So I opened my mouth and said, "There are also male feminists."

This came as a shock to them, and they started in with homo jokes, men who want to be women. So I started to question whether I was a male feminist. My decision was that I was not. I believe in equality, but I also believe that a true male feminist is someone who speaks up for women. The kind of person who is not afraid. At this point in my life, I am not prepared to go out and do this. I know I am copping out. But right now I am hoping just to make it through college, not change minds and feelings. I hope I will someday, at a later date, build the courage to speak out.

Male students were—and are—subjected to constant peer skepticism about their masculinity once they enroll in women's history. Girlfriends as well as buddies insisted these students would quickly "turn gay" after a month in my class. Both mothers and fathers berated sons for taking women's studies, although in some families female relatives, including aunts, grandmothers, and sisters offered support and encouragement. Male students buoyed by the inspiration of strong women in their own lives brought confidence to the classroom, and they were able to write thoughtfully about the mixed notions of normal heterosexual behavior. One male student wrote a paper about the slurs his female classmates endured, pointing out that a heterosexual student identifying herself as a feminist might be called a "dyke," while another, insisting she could not be a feminist because she liked men, was labeled a "slut." He found campus examples where visibly activist females were accused of being both a dyke and a slut, simultaneously.

I have a scrapbook full of cards and e-mails from former male students who say that my classes changed them forever. It's painful to compare the welcome mat they found outside my door with the harsh backlash from their own (male) best friends. But I include their class conversations from over the years to ask, again: Who's doing the male bashing? The majority of put-downs seem to come from other guys, not my textbooks.

Once my male students were comfortable enough to speak up in the women's studies classroom, their comments added important points of view. Quite often, male students saw females as extra privileged, as beneficiaries of a looks-based double standard on college campuses. They cited female peers who used tears and feminine charm to beg male professors for deadline extensions on late papers. Young men from affluent backgrounds, in whose families women controlled the wealth, property, and inheritance decisions, found it especially difficult to see female college peers as emblematic of historical "oppression" in any way. Indeed, they noted the extra social cushions around women of wealth, who appeared both protected and empowered. In male students' written work, a common theme was the concept of a reverse discrimination favoring women on campus: drinking parties that welcomed underage women (but not men), escort services for women who felt threatened late at night (but not men), police who excused traffic violations by cute women (but not men). This perceived favoritism angered male students whose own freewheeling moments were punished, deservedly or not, by authorities. Although most white male students were spared the specific humiliations reserved for African American males their age—routine demands for identification, being stopped by police looking for "suspicious" intruders in college buildings, and so forth—most young men in the high-profile 18- to 22-year-old demographic, hovering at legal drinking age, felt they were too often presumed guilty while female peers could sob touchingly and go free. These candid assessments contrasted sharply with some female students' accounts of, for instance, the sexual pawing they encountered at drinking parties; free admission is not always free.

One male student expressed his frustration with feminism by starting a discussion with "Let me tell you how good women have it." He felt women could party to excess without repercussion because his own female friends did not expect to earn their own living after graduation—or ever—and could thus let their grades slide. Their option of marrying well and avoiding the working world altogether, he suggested, meant that women as a group did not face men's pressures to succeed financially.

Plenty of male students saw themselves as playing a critical role straddling the fence in campus debates on feminism. They defended my classes to jeering friends, were honest about the problem of underreported date rape, and some went out of their way to attend female athletes' games, cheering loudly. But in contrast to female classmates, most male students were not as invested in defending a *curriculum* on women. They were simply relieved to find that classwork in women's studies was not, as they had feared, a politically correct trap designed to disadvantage them.

I came in a skeptic and I have been pleasantly surprised.

I can honestly say that after taking your class
I see many things in a new light.

I am the kid you met at the airport and invited to take a women's studies class. I am so glad you did. I went out and read your book!!!

Dr. Morris, I would not miss a single one of your lectures except I ruptured my eardrum and also keep throwing up.

Do not think of me as a faceless name. I truly enjoy class.

I knew right away you would be super cool and I
totally appreciate all you have taught me.

I would be a fool not to take your class. People like
you are the reason I'm headed to college.

If it's important to acknowledge all the terrific male students who take women's history classes and thrive, it's also necessary to remember the role that women play in mocking women's studies. Some college women do poke fun at male students who take women's studies courses, often with homophobic slurs; and women from conservative student groups play key roles in questioning the necessity of academic feminism. Some female students will interview me before deciding whether to enroll in a course, bringing in checklists of questions to determine if I offer balanced views, even occasionally subjecting me to really ill-mannered interrogations. They are supported in this behavior by organizations such as Accuracy in Academia, Campus Watch, and the Center for the Study of Popular Culture, which once funded UCLA alumni to monitor faculty perceived as left-leaning by tape recording their lectures (resulting in a list called the "Dirty Thirty"). Urging students to identify and avoid liberal faculty, in 2006 David Horowitz published *The Professors: The 101 Most Dangerous Academics in America* (I'm not one of them).

One young woman at Georgetown, uncertain whether or not to register for my class, introduced herself by demanding, "Do you regularly silence your male students or allow female classmates to berate them? Are you able to provide me with a list of your publications, should you have any?" Even after examining my course syllabi, she was convinced a women's studies professor must be, at heart, a male-bashing dilettante. I told her that there were other ways to get to know me than by impugning my professionalism at the first handshake. What is maddening is that somewhere, behind the right-wing backlash, is a vaguely stated concern for "traditional values"—which, one would hope, might include respect for a teacher, or for an adult woman. But since both print media and talk radio activists have increasingly employed outright rudeness as a means of political scrutiny, too many students feel entitled to belittle professors whose courses suggest any concessions to feminism (historic, academic, modern).

One wearies of reassuring critics that there is no "bashing" going on in the women's history classroom, just plain old studying. Yes, I often have to reassure young men like Ralph that learning about women won't kill you. But many are the male students who take up the challenge and, after a semester of hard work, come by my office to thank me.

With Supreme Court Justice Sandra Day O'Connor,
on the set of the Richard Karz film *If Women
Ruled the World,* at the U.S. Capitol, 1999

6.

Scene Six, 1990
Driving a U-Haul to Harvard

YES! YES! YES! I've been offered a one-year appointment as a visiting scholar in women's studies at Harvard.

I spend an exuberant, conceited, reckless afternoon telephoning everyone who ever doubted me, who ever taunted me, who ever told me I'd go nowhere if I pursued women's history. "A Harvard professor at 28!" I scream down the phone at old enemies and ex-lovers. I bounce off the walls of my house, ride my mountain bike in circles in the parking lot, eat all my favorite foods at once: latkes, sour cream, Greek olives, a pineapple milkshake. I'll be the youngest visiting scholar at Harvard Divinity School and the first-ever to teach a graduate seminar on Jewish women's history. Everything has been worth it, now; everything. And my father calls, saying, "Bon, I was one of those who thought women's studies wouldn't get you anywhere. And now I stand corrected."

Yep, that was a pretty fun day. But now . . . now I have to move from northern California, where I had my first teaching job, across the United States to Cambridge, Massachusetts . . . with all my worldly possessions in a U-Haul attached to my ten-year-old Toyota. And the Toyota has a starter problem. It starts exactly once a day, then won't start again if you dare to turn it off. I'm driving ten, eleven, twelve hours a day, alone, through the 107-degree heat wave in the Great West that summer, pulling up to gas stations and throwing gas into the tank with the motor running, racing away until dusk approaches and I've picked out a cheap motel. Then, parking, I turn off the motor, and the next morning, I start the car again.

I do this for 3,000 miles. And, along the way, I learn what people really think about a woman traveling alone.

Halfway across America, I pull into Princeton, Illinois—birthplace of Ronald Reagan. It's the week of July 4th, and when I try to check in at a motel, the woman at the desk chirps, "If you're wearing red, white, and blue, I'll give you two dollars off!"

I'm exhausted, sunburned, grimy. All I want is a room, and an ice bucket to stick my head in. But an equally grimy Texas trucker has arrived at the same time, and, assuming we're a couple, the woman at the desk asks if we'd like the king-size bed.

"Ma'am," I say, "I'm not with him."

She looks at me with suspicion. "You're alone? Single? No husband? Not married?"

"Not married, traveling alone."

She's never heard of such a thing, and looks distastefully at my sweaty driving clothes. "You'd better hurry up and get married, honey; from the looks of you, you sure aren't getting any younger."

In the motel room, when I lift the lid of the toilet, there's a pepperoni on the seat. Just one. I'm glad I looked before I sat. Clearly the room was not quite cleaned after some guest's pizza party; or is this an eerie welcome gift? The downscale version of fancier inns leaving a mint on your pillow?

Six states later, I'm almost in Boston—just eleven miles to go—when I hear a loud explosion behind me; a flat tire on the U-Haul. Although I do know how to change a tire, and unpack everything from my Toyota to get my tools, my spare tire won't fit the U-Haul rim, and after all that, I have to flag down a highway repairman on the Massachusetts Turnpike.

The repairman takes one look at my California license plates and shudders. "Lord!" he says, "I sure wouldn't want to live out there—with all those gay people, you know." He's holding a tire jack in his calloused hands, and we're alone by the side of the road, but I'm too tired to think of a polite lie; I snap out the first thought that comes to me, uncensored. "Aw, you're looking at one, bub! Not so scary, am I?"

He's flabbergasted. "You! You're a—a homosexual person?" he gasps. I nod.

"But—you're a woman!" he points out. I nod again.

"Well, gee. Not to get personal or anything.
But, like—what is it that two women do?"

"Can we change the tire, first?" I request. But he's really impressed now. He asks if he can shake my hand. It's like meeting a celebrity, for him: a real live homo, and she's friendly! I've made his day. He's going to tell this story to all his drinking buddies. So we change the tire together, and I talk to him a bit about gay rights. He's taking it all in, listening. Even there, broken down and stranded on the freeway, I've started my new job as a Harvard professor. This man is my first student.

This scene is all about measuring up to others' expectations, ideals, and stereotypes. Most of my old friends, former classmates, skeptical relatives, and even total strangers who snickered at my choice of a women's studies career abruptly changed their tune when they learned I'd been hired at Harvard: *Oh! Well! That's a real job, then!* I was amazed to see how Harvard's seal of approval suddenly legitimized women's studies for those who had found the field laughable only minutes before. I, too, had to examine how a one-year appointment brought all my own internalized doubts up to the surface: *If Harvard wants me, it's proof that my work matters. But will I be able to fit in? Am I smart enough?*

Every woman friend I'd known in graduate school had, at one time or another, confessed this fear of unworthiness: *Did they make a mistake in admitting me to Ph.D. candidacy? Am I really smart?* All of us were heavily invested in the very feminist history that showed how institutions like Harvard had deliberately kept women out. Yet a Harvard appointment "confirmed" our intelligence, our worth. We were that shaky in our confidence as scholars. As one of my new Harvard graduate students later remarked to me, "If my work is critical of male power, language, and definitions, why do I look to rewards from male institutions and authority figures as proof of my work's value? Why is approval from my feminist peers not sufficiently validating?"

At the same time, understanding academic sexism and how Ivy League institutions had systematically excluded female role models placed a unique burden on me to challenge Harvard norms. I would be charged with hammering feminist perspectives onto those musty Ivy League walls; many were the well-wishers who told me, "Give 'em hell up there," or "Shake up that campus," or "Remember, we're all counting on you to change the face of the good-old-boy network in academia." And while I worried privately that I might not know how to behave appropriately in an Ivy League setting, working-class friends warned me not to become a snob who'd look down on them. Opinions and expectations flew at me like darts from every direction—but at least these were critics and supporters who believed that women's studies belonged in Harvard classrooms.

Traveling across the country, though, alone behind the wheel with my thoughts about the coming Harvard year, I was simply a woman without a man; a spinster on the road. As the scene in the play points out, I was forced to explain or defend my single status all along the way, even pressed into a haphazard coming-out moment in the breakdown lane near Boston. Those incidents are fun to re-enact, because of course the U-Haul journey had a happy ending. I really did get to be, just once, a Harvard professor. For so much of Ivy League history, I would not have even been allowed to enroll as a Harvard student.

In 2005, Houghton Mifflin published Berkeley professor Jerome Karabel's 700-page volume, *The Chosen: The Hidden History of Admission and Exclusion at Harvard, Yale, and Princeton.* Karabel's research showed, in detail, a systematic history of Ivy League exclusionary practices. Admissions criteria were formed and enforced by a powerful Protestant elite—educated men, yes, but ones who believed with all their hearts that only other white, Protestant males from a specific wellspring of elite preparatory schools and old families possessed the leadership and character America needed. Athletic ability and alumni family connections could, more often than not, compensate for low test scores. But Harvard's leading men did not believe women, Jews, or homosexuals, regardless of outstanding academic merit, had sufficient character to make their admission worthwhile.

Consider these quotes from Karabel: "Lowell was also no friend to the education of women. In response to a casual suggestion that the law school become coeducational, he kicked the door in his office and declared stonily, 'This isn't going to happen while I am president of this university'" (49). Or: "When Lowell discovered that a longtime member of the Harvard faculty was homosexual, he immediately demanded his resignation. But the professor pointed out that he had devoted his life to Harvard and asked Lowell what he would do if he were in his shoes. Lowell's reply, corroborated by two sources, was direct: 'I would get a gun and shoot myself'" (50). And: "To Lowell, Harvard's rising Jewish enrollment posed a threat . . . making it imperative to bring the 'Jewish invasion' under control. . . . Lowell explained that his main concern was that the sheer number of Jews would cause the flight of the Protestant elite and thereby 'ruin the college'" (88). Ouch.

And then there's William Wright's book *Harvard's Secret Court: The Savage 1920 Purge of Campus Homosexuals.* In 2007, accepting the annual leadership award for outstanding service to the gay community (presented by Harvard's present-day Gay and Lesbian Caucus), the education activist Kevin Jennings dedicated his speech to the memory of Eugene Cummings, "who was accused of being gay and [was] informed at an administrative board meeting in 1920 that he would be expelled from Harvard, at which point he went back to his room and killed himself."[1]

Thus burdened with history, I walked into my new home as scholar-in-residence at Currier House with a box of Indigo Girls and Alix Dobkin cassettes under one arm, and a manuscript-in-progress on Jewish feminism in my patch-covered backpack. I was young, gay, Jewish, and female, with a Harvard faculty ID card—my ancestors and various affiliated communities of identity all whispering, "You go, girl!" in my ear. I stood in the hallway for a minute, keenly aware of those founding fathers who would never have allowed me to belong, whose portraits frowned down on me from every wall. Then I turned the key in the lock of my new door and moved in.

In 1990, it was one thing to be invited to teach women's studies at Harvard Divinity School—a bastion of progressive compassion and liberal activism. But the rest of Harvard debated and snarled over the place of women's studies in academia; plenty of faculty, including government professor Harvey Mansfield, were vocally opposed to the Women's Studies Program. The late Carolyn Heilbrun, who took her own life after decades of battling Ivy League sexism, portrayed Harvard's hostile climate toward women in the murder mystery *Death in a Tenured Position* (written under the pseudonym Amanda Cross). Within my first month, as I waited in the faculty lounge of the English department for a colleague, a male professor challenged my presence. Assuming I did not belong, he informed me that, ahem, only faculty were permitted in "his" lounge. When I produced my faculty ID card, he labored to save face by harrumphing, "But you look too young and pretty to be a professor. Now, isn't that a compliment, my dear?" I heard variations on this theme throughout my entire year at Harvard. Meanwhile, a more common and more degrading ex-

---

1. Kevin Jennings, "Lessons from a Witch Hunt of the 1920s," *The Gay and Lesbian Review* 14 (Sept.–Oct. 2007): 5.

perience, for black students and faculty, was to be stopped by security guards and asked for identification. Mentors to black students advised them to wear a backpack or sweatshirt with the Harvard logo whenever crossing campus, particularly at night.

If women have been made to feel unwelcome, uninvited, in the most elite institutions of higher education, then of course it's no surprise that women's history should also be an unwelcome latecomer in some Ivy League classrooms. What women do during their lives has rarely been entered into the record, receiving little scrutiny in books by and about Great Men. That women willingly help make great men great, and willingly participate in excluding themselves and other women from the record, is a messy topic. To this day, women make up the majority of K–12 teachers and daycare workers, supervising the majority of U.S. classroom spaces where kids are first exposed to lessons about whose history counts. But somehow, this division of labor hasn't made elementary schools into feminist landscapes, or even gender-neutral ones. The power to keep school curricula focused on male achievement has a lot to do with male superintendents, principals, and textbook authors, the ever-widening administrative circles of men just beyond female teachers' classroom doors.

This pattern has long ruled our American education system. By the mid-nineteenth century, teaching was identifiable as a female profession—although a badly paying one and, as a career, the last resort for a spinster, lending both stigma and pity to the poor unmarried "schoolmarm." Because many public schools would only employ single women (forcing female teachers to resign after marrying) and private academies for girls might hire nuns as teaching faculty, an association grew between scholarly women and asexuality or celibacy. Female teachers might be accomplished in learning, yet somehow, what mattered was how they had failed as ordinary women. Physicians obsessed over the low marriage and childbirth rates of studious women; the fact that some dedicated female educators were by no means asexual, but thriving in long-term lesbian relationships, was simply not discussed. (Lillian Faderman's award-winning research, presented in books such as *Surpassing the Love of Men* and *To Believe in Women,* investigates the hitherto suppressed history of same-sex love in the nineteenth century.)

Although women were eventually recruited to teach kindergarten through high school, during most of the nineteenth-century college faculty were men: men who could and did set barriers for college-ambitious women. Edward H. Clarke, a Harvard Medical School professor, was a champion of the late nineteenth-century theory that higher education for women would ruin their reproductive systems; his 1873 volume *Sex in Education* warned that "identical education of the two sexes is a crime before God and humanity that physiology protests against." Separate and unequal education prevailed. Separate and unequal—in endowment, facilities, and curriculum—were Radcliffe to Harvard and Barnard to Columbia. Yet the Seven Sisters offered as elite an education as a nineteenth-century woman could find: if she were, of course white, Protestant, rich.[2]

What men/husbands in positions of power feared was the sterility of educated women. Supposedly, hard study used up women's limited energy and redirected their meager blood supply from womb to brain. More likely, a college education granted women access to two main professions, teaching and nursing, which not incidentally required that women remain single as a condition for employment. It appears that more than half of Smith College graduates in the late nineteenth century, for instance, did not marry or have children. White leaders saw this trend as "race suicide"—the daughters of America's more affluent classes were not reproducing, or not reproducing as rapidly as their African American or immigrant sisters. If educated motherhood was a plus for the nation, some educated women's choices to limit family size sparked genuine fear. And this fear has by no means vanished: Today, in 2009, when women outnumber men at college campuses throughout the United States, news articles abound on whether these smart gals will ever find husbands. There has also been an accompanying trend of books and essays on how women's present academic success threatens men with "reverse discrimination," a topic I'll return to later.

Once women began attending the same colleges as men—or pursuing equivalent degrees at women's colleges—rules and recommendations for their behavior on campus abounded. Men struggled to date college women within the labyrinth of regulations; much of mid-twentieth-century college humor dealt with the delicate issue of co-education. *Where the Girls Are,* published by the Daily Princetonian in 1965 as "A Social Guide to Women's Colleges in the East," had the following reports on women's elite institutions: "Bryn Mawr is perhaps the most self-consciously intellectual of all the Seven Sisters. . . .

---

2. The Seven Sisters refers to seven elite, private northeastern colleges for women established in the late nineteenth century: Barnard, Bryn Mawr, Mount Holyoke, Radcliffe, Smith, Vassar, and Wellesley. Barnard has retained its distinction as separate from Columbia University, while Radcliffe eventually merged with Harvard.

While the Bryn Mawr lass may try hard to show that she is just-one-of-the-girls, it is still the man prepared to discuss existentialism and Romantic poetry who will get along best with her." The following page includes a cartoon of a gangly and bespectacled Bryn Mawrter reading Kant. "Goucher girls are still waiting to be discovered by Eastern men, so they have to be more outgoing than their Seven Sisters counterparts, and a little easier to snow." (But how outgoing could one be with a 10:30 PM curfew on weeknights?) The presumably more bohemian Mount Holyoke girl was drawn barefoot, in slacks and a turtleneck, clutching a beer while riding a skateboard. It was even more hip to be at Sarah Lawrence: That cartoon depicted a stereotypical folksinger in peasant blouse, fishnet stockings, giant black sunglasses, and hoop earrings, carrying a guitar.

And then there's Smith College—the very institution parents were warned to avoid in the late nineteenth century if they wanted their daughters to reproduce for the affluent classes. According to *Where the Girls Are,* even seventy-five years later a Smithie was still defined by her marital prospects or lack thereof: "The smug, overly happy ones who are going to be married shortly after graduation; and the worried, nervous ones who haven't even been pinned. Always keep in mind that a Smithie is looking at you not only as her date but also as the man who may some day be footing the bills to send her daughter to Smith." At least these man-hungry, education-minded singles weren't at risk for the superstitions dominating Wheaton College: "Tradition says that if a girl walks under the circle of light cast by the lamp in the archway, she is doomed to the life of an old maid."

Why no mention of Radcliffe women? They were dismissed with just one, devastating paragraph: "Radcliffe students are probably the most intelligent of the Eastern women's colleges. Even outside of Cambridge's multiple coffee houses, you can still tell a 'Cliffie a block away. She wears a dirty trench coat (it would be "out" to have it washed) and long hair (same reason)."

Lynn Peril's 2006 book *College Girls* pokes fun at this herstory. Peril covers the range of advice literature aimed at Ivy League women, from fashion makeovers to specific product ads that insulted brainy girls while nonetheless luring them in as potential consumers. The important rule was not to fall behind in fashion while advancing in knowledge. One hundred years of ads and essays mocking unattractive scholars helped keep many an Ivy League woman insecure, apologetic—a quality I was startled to find among the graduate students I met at Harvard in 1990.

I expected, at Harvard, to be overwhelmed and intimidated by women more brilliant than I'd ever met before. Frequently, I was. But I also heard, in the graduate seminar I taught and in other faculty classes I attended as a guest, the inevitable lack of confidence from women who were sure Harvard had somehow erred in admitting them to graduate school. My notes from that year include these quotes from their conversations:

How will we speak up in class? One of our constructed virtues as women is to let other people go first.

And while everyone in the room may speak, not everyone is HEARD. What are our qualities as listeners?

How do we talk about other women without generalizing, objectifying them all over again? Can we treat other women's lives as sacred texts?

As women at Harvard we have a simultaneously limited and privileged position from which to speak. We feel we must obey the institution which extends us the privilege of access. We are so new to power.

Some men feel that admitting women to Harvard has lowered the prestige of the university. They may feel the same way about bringing women's history into a history program.

We are leery of institutions we've been excluded from, but if we want a woman-friendly environment, we need to gain positions of visibility and control.

We spend so much of our time justifying women's studies, pleading for its inclusion, rather than working.

Why is the history of women, and African Americans, belittled as "the focus of special interest groups"?

To professionalize our field, are we avoiding translating information on women's history into stories accessible to everyone? What do we disguise with "academese"?

Postmodernism won't get information on women's lives and histories to women outside of academic networks. We have to be bilingual, using the language of feminist scholarship and of feminist street activism as well.

Women without access to institutional power do have knowledge: of damage, of ways to circumvent oppression through mutual support. Every woman is an expert on womanhood. But we establish authenticity through personal experience. Academia relies on the scientific method.

There is so much we don't know about women's lives. "Accurate" historical "facts" are based on the male record. Women's history scholarship threatens men because we unmask their "expertise," revealing how limited it is.

There is a new relationship between knowledge and group identity. But in most societies, women are not organized enough to respond with unified voices.

The male body is always the norm. Women may get "equal rights" with men, but we can't use those rights because we're busy raising men's kids. We become women on the occasions when we bleed: menarche, loss of virginity, childbirth. Men become men when they spill blood: ours, animals', other men's.

The danger is declaring, "I'm a victim, therefore my story has value." It teaches us to identify with pain, not power, as our primary shared resource. Can we avoid bonding around victimization?

These notes reflect shared concerns among top female scholars at Harvard Divinity School in 1990. Some of us returned, briefly, in February of 2005, when HDS celebrated "Fifty Years of Women" with an ingathering of past students and faculty from its Women's Studies in Religion program. During the day of speeches, receptions, and glad reunions, the longtime director of the women's studies program, Dr. Constance Buchanan, revealed that many high-achieving female students had come to her over the years with the refrain "I just don't feel like I belong here." So many had struggled to see their lives and their realities in the overwhelmingly male environment.

Ultimately, we emerged from Harvard Yard having honed new skills as advocates for women's history. Today, in my own classes, I'm proud to use texts written by other women who did their research while at HDS: Bernadette Brooten, R. Marie Griffith, Ann Braude, Reverend Irene Monroe, Ann Pellegrini. The two books I wrote myself, during that one-year appointment, were also published. But all of us, despite having "made it to the show" (as my baseball-loving pal Doug put it), spent part of our magic time at Harvard worrying if we were worthy of the opportunity, at all. The problem of confidence haunts our sex.

Fortunately, recent events have shaken up Harvard in ways we never dreamed. A few years after the controversial remarks by the then president Lawrence Summers, who famously declared that biological differences might account for women lagging behind men in the sciences, Harvard appointed a woman as its 28th president, effective July 1, 2007. The historian Drew Gilpin Faust now leads Harvard in this new century of change and female power.

אוניברסיטת תל-אביב

הפורום ללימודי נשים

הפורום ללימודי נשים, החוג הצעיר

בשיתוף עם קל"ף, קהילה לסבית פמיניסטית

מזמינים להצגתה של

Professor Bonnie J. Morris

Revenge of the Women's Studies Professor

אשר תתקיים ביום חמישי, ה-10 ביוני בשעה 19:00, בבניין גילמן, חדר 326

בתום ההצגה יתקיים דיון

ההצגה תתחיל בשעה 19:00 בדיוק

Poster for a performance at Tel Aviv University in Israel, 1999

7.

Scene Seven, 1992
Fear of the Word *Woman*

Harvard was wonderful. A year of prestige, wine and cheese receptions in grand hallways, string quartets playing as I walked in my regalia through the Yard. Of course, many departments at formerly all-male Harvard were still getting used to women and people of color on the faculty. There was that angry older professor who asked to see my ID when he found me reading in the faculty lounge. I had to prove that I belonged.

Then came the recession, and no one offered me a job. I had nowhere to go from that wonderful year but down.

It's been months without work, and all my money is gone. Now I live in one room without a bathtub or an oven, counting pennies, writing articles, sending out my resume. I'm actually mistaken for a homeless woman and asked to leave a posh store in Harvard Square. New colleagues from last year forget about me, embarrassed that I'm unemployed; when I see my Harvard students I run away before they can invite me to have lunch. I can't afford to eat where they'll invite me.

What happened to the women's studies field? Budget cuts and backlash. It's hard to find a job when schools are cutting corners; multiculturalism is a dirty word right now. Women's history is a luxury some schools cannot afford—although I notice football budgets rarely are decreased. My friends say, "Bon, just keep writing. Pretend you've won a grant. This is your writing year." They're right: Everything I write that year gets published; three books that come out later. But I can't eat my words.

One hundred and eight job applications later,
I'm finally invited to interview for a women's history
position at a conservative Midwestern college.

Ten different men interrogate me. Every half hour I'm
ushered into a different male professor's office and questioned
about how I'll fit in here. Some openly laugh at me. Finally, I
beg to meet the one woman on the faculty. She invites me into
her office, locks the door, bursts into tears, throws herself into
my arms and sobs, "Oh, God, do we need you here!" Then
I'm sent to meet with some students—history majors.

The students, too, are all male—and, for some reason, very
angry with me. "I suppose you know," says one, "how disappointed
we are that the college would conduct a women's history search,
instead of hiring a scholar who can teach us fundamentals." I
ask what he means by fundamentals, and he explains, "Well,
perhaps ancient history. Real history, of some kind." Were there
no women alive in ancient Greece, or Rome? No women in the
biblical era? No queens, goddesses, pharaohs? No Helen of Troy,
no Athena, no Sappho? Is our heritage so unreal? But this guy
isn't interested in what I know, or what I might have to offer.
Rather, in front of his peers and other faculty, he tells me why I'm
not a real scholar. When I mention this incident to the department
chair, he chuckles that some people do find Dave "aggressive."

Finally we get down to the pressing matter of what courses
I might teach. I'm really prepared, excited, presenting my syllabi
and outlines for courses like Women and Work, Women and
War, Women in American Political History. But the chairman
seems unhappy. He fumbles, "Now, look. Say. Do you think, ah,
that you could change the titles of these classes? See, there's
a problem. They all have the word *woman* in the title."

Because I'm interviewing for a job advertised as women's
history, I'm puzzled by his complaint. But he tells me that the
word *woman* in a course catalogue might turn off some of the
male students, and we can't have that. Don't I see his point?

I draw a deep breath. Oh, how I need this job! I picture
my empty bank account, my apartment with no bathtub, my
30th birthday looming up ahead. Gently, I explain that sure, I
could shift around some wording. I can call this course Sex
Roles in American History or Work and Family in American
History, but each course is really about women. I suggest,

as respectfully as possible, that the chairman is offering me advice similar to what children's book authors hear: Always make the main character a boy, to increase sales! Girls will read books about little boys, but boys won't pick up a book about a girl. Just make the boy the main character in the story!

The history chairman scratches his head. "I guess I see your point," he says. I smile, and we shake hands. Later, I learn they've cancelled the position entirely and called it a "failed search." In short, they'd rather have nobody than hire me.

Fear of the word *woman.*

Can you imagine a job search for a professor of Asian history where the candidate is told to keep the word *Asian* out of course titles, lest it intimidate white students? A professor of Middle Eastern history being directed to substitute the word *Western*? A scholar in Judaic studies ordered to advertise her courses as Christian History? And yet, throughout the 1990s, I was told that "calling it women's history will scare students away."

This piece in my play is really about the job market, and the desperate search for a tenure-track position that all new Ph.D.s undertake. I came into academia just at the moment when tenured positions were beginning to vanish, supplanted by adjunct appointments. More and more undergraduate teaching passed into the hands of part-time faculty, hired per course, at a flat rate, without benefits or the possibility of promotion. Very few women's studies programs were able to make tenure-track appointments, as most were indeed *programs* and not *departments.* A program might have a director, whereas a department had a chair. A women's studies director might be tenured in a humanities or social science department while overseeing a women's studies program for the university, perhaps one leading to a minor or a certificate. The director might have funding to hire one or two visiting professors, but primarily assembled a core women's studies curriculum from courses already being taught in the university: say, Women in Medieval History, Women in Literature, Women and International Development. Such courses, if offered regularly by the History, English, and Economics faculty, could count toward women's studies credits. Using this method cost universities next to nothing to create a women's studies minor. Little has changed: See the 2007 National Census of Women's and Gender Studies Programs in U.S. Institutions of Higher Education, available online or from the National Women's Studies Association.

Creating a major, however, meant offering additional prerequisite courses like Introduction to Women's Studies and Feminist Theory, and perhaps hiring instructors for two- or three-year appointments. These were the jobs, advertised nationwide, to which I hopefully applied. But I also applied for tenure-track history positions, which advertised a search for a women's history specialist. And those were the interviews where history program administrators revealed their obvious discomfort with women.

During the initial five years of my teaching career, when like so many young faculty I was an academic nomad moving from one short-term appointment to another, I probably applied for almost three hundred history positions. Only once did a female professor interview me. The dramatic backlash against affirmative action in that era, 1989–94, with conservative scholars railing against the political correctness of hiring more female and minority candidates, effectively convinced many people outside of academia that the Ivory Tower had been "taken over." I even heard hints of this sentiment from a good friend, who sighed, "You know, it's really hard for a white male to get work now." She feared for the prospects of her male partner, who today is the head of a prestigious history department, while both she and I remain untenured women's studies adjuncts. My experience in the job market was that men had no difficulty getting work.

I was always interviewed by men: male department chairs, male deans, male students. At every university where I was eventually employed, the male history faculty outnumbered the women by an enormous margin: eleven to three, eighteen to two. The scene I recreated for my play was just one actual interview experience. Others were equally bizarre.

A dean poised to say yea or nay to my appointment leaned toward me, sighing, "Do you really think we're going to *need* women's history five years from now?"

At another interview, I was taken to lunch at a local restaurant, and the campus minister walked in. Only seeing me from the back—I was seated at a table surrounded by male faculty from the history program—he mistook me for the daughter of one of those professors, and came up behind me, kissing the top of my head with a loud smack and a fond, "Hiya, Sugar!"

On another occasion, I interviewed for and won a small research grant, based on my dissertation work. The grant was named for a woman who had willed her estate to help worthy students, and her brother served as executor of the will. When he arrived to hand over the check, he looked at me with suspicion and demanded, "Wait. You aren't some kind of a feminist, are you?" "Well, yes, sir, I am," I replied truthfully, plucking the check from his fingers with my most charming smile. That was the moment the photographer captured.

I had to charm—or convince—many a dean that women's studies was in the best interests of his students, and here's what always worked. *I had to explain that a course in women's history would help young men get jobs.* Stating the obvious—that women are half the world's population, are rapidly outnumbering men on American campuses, and have experiences and contributions worth studying from a scholarly, social science perspective—only served to inflate fear of feminist rhetoric invading the classroom.

By the mid-1990s, however, the United States was beginning to awaken to global oppression of women. Pointing to the myriad opportunities available to women in America vs. those available to, say, women in Afghanistan made even the most conservative men feel proud. Negotiating gender etiquette in Japan or Saudi Arabia would be essential for an ambitious business major; no one would dispute that separate social spheres for male and female pervaded Middle Eastern society. Understanding the actual laws and practices of Islam, as they applied to men and women, suddenly became an essential range of knowledge for any political science major. And men who expected to succeed as managers would be employing working mothers: a course or two on workplace policy couldn't hurt. In-depth familiarity with sexual harassment law could stave off an expensive, embarrassing lawsuit. This was the pitch that often convinced deans: Women's studies would help young men to gain power.

It was painful to direct my "sales pitch" in this way, but I needed a job.

Meanwhile, mainstream American media didn't support my argument that global women's issues mattered. For example, in fall 1995, when the Fourth U.N. World Conference on Women met in China to draft a major document on women's rights, almost no coverage appeared on American television, not even when the then First Lady Hillary Rodham Clinton gave a keynote speech on the global struggle for women's education and equality. Instead, networks bumped her speech—"Women's rights are human rights. Among those rights are the *right to speak freely—and the right to be heard!*"—so that the evening news could celebrate the birthday of baseball legend Cal Ripken.[1] No matter how I argued that a focus on women's history would benefit men as world leaders, popular media demonstrated that men's sports outweighed women's

---

1. Hillary Rodham Clinton's speech is available in audio and text format at http://www.americanrhetoric.com/speeches/hillaryclintonbeijingspeech.htm (accessed June 7, 2008). For an alternative perspective on Clinton's Beijing visit, see *Beyond Beijing: The International Women's Movement,* produced and directed by Salome Chasnoff (videocassette; Evanston, Ill.: Distributed by Salome Chasnoff/Beyond Media, 1996).

rights as world news. (This was one factor in my choice, later that year, to develop a sports history class.)

When I enjoyed a prestigious appointment at Harvard as a young scholar, the idea that I might be out of work afterwards never occurred to me, or to my parents and friends. It was mortifying to go directly from Harvard to unemployment, and to watch my savings vanish as I spent a year applying for jobs in a climate ambivalent about my field. But it also never occurred to me to give up teaching women's studies as the way I earned my bread. I might never be rich, but I would live my beliefs. Feminist labor historian Alice Kessler-Harris, one of my professors in graduate school, had written in her introduction to Anzia Yezierska's novel *The Bread Givers* that in the eyes of many Jewish women immigrants, "America held out the promise of love and satisfying work." I wanted that.

Could one live on an adjunct instructor's salary? Kinda. Sorta. Mostly. How would I explain to my loved ones how little I was earning, teaching part-time at Northeastern University without benefits as I searched for that ever-distant tenure-track job? For a year I embodied and romanticized bohemian living. I was a starving artist living in a studio, teaching part-time while writing two different books. I had spent six years of graduate school in a town where a $5,500 teaching assistantship covered the rent of a two-bedroom apartment with sun porch and mountain views. I knew how to live well on almost nothing, and I had retained control of my work in one important way: No one told me what to put in my class syllabus. Teaching part-time left room for activism, bookstore readings, offering workshops at women's music festivals, and staging my first attempt at a one-woman play, *Passing*.

Did I want to be a beloved but poor writer, without health insurance, reading poetry in a dimly lit café by night, mentoring wide-eyed students by day? Yes and no. Yes and no. It was easy to "float" for a bit in a city like Boston, chockablock with university students and young visiting scholars at various stages of career, everyone wearing a patched backpack, everyone's evenings crammed like PBS stations with talks by provocative intellectuals at different campus institutions, and enough wine and cheese at any event to count as dinner four nights out of seven. But I had *been* that visiting intellectual, showcased at Harvard, protected for a year. Was there nowhere to go but downhill?

What did I say to colleagues I met at wine-and-cheese receptions? If my students were blissfully unaware, indifferent to the salaries and status hierarchies of faculty, snubs and queries from colleagues still had the power to demoralize and hurt. "Part-timer? Oh. So, do you have any plans to move on?

Are you looking for a *real* job?" This forced me to choose between (A) disclosing the huge number of jobs I had applied for that year alone or (B) daring to assert that one could be happy and thrive in a nontenured context, thanks. If anyone had asked, "What are you writing?" I'd have been at ease in a wink, able to talk for hours on equal footing. This never happened.

Too often, I heard the starkest, rudest inquiry of all: "How do you live?"—or the more imperative, "But you can't live on that!"

Here is how one lives on an adjunct salary: carefully. It is a lifestyle similar to that of any other professor in most ways: a schedule including reading, writing, lecturing, grading, photocopying, forming lasting ties to students and colleagues, giving papers at conferences, publishing, thinking, traveling, eating, sleeping—just on a tiny budget. The brain teaser is having rather prestigious social standing (a college professor!) while drawing working-class pay (requiring financial aid to attend conferences). If one truly loves education, one may live joyfully, too, but without frills.

Over the years, I have taught women's history on an adjunct contract while enjoying a high quality of life. Consider that a feminist scholar's main needs and expenses are satisfied by basic university affiliation: computer access, free e-mail, laser printing, paper, envelopes, outgoing mail, long-distance calls, pens, disks, paper clips. Then there's the access to athletic facilities. Some universities charge all faculty expensive gym fees, but at others I had free use of a huge swimming pool, an ice hockey arena, aerobics and kickboxing courses. And then there are the free desk copies of new books. Oh, baby. Delicious new books, year-round.

I don't smoke, drink more than once a month, cook meat at home, or have other expensive habits. In my adjunct years, I perfected the healthy, inexpensive grocery list: one loaf of challah: $2.39. Tomatoes, spinach, red leaf lettuce, and two bell peppers: $9. That was lunch for a week. Free coffee came from my faculty lounge; my one vice was cinnamon coffee creamer: $2.50 a week. Orange juice: $3. Bananas and yoghurt: $10. That was breakfast for a week. Dinner for a week: in Boston I was allowed to dine twice a week at Currier House, and at least one night a week I went to some presentation with a hearty reception spread. The rest of the week I dined on broccoli, rice, tofu, spinach, sweet potatoes, zucchini, angel hair pasta, and the occasional salmon splurge; my snacks were matzos or carrots with hummus dip, or a cup of chai. Toiletries, ink cartridges for my beloved Sheaffer fountain pen, and subway change completed my monthly budget. I had a fantastic old car, the Toyota I'd crossed the country with, and in summer I did work exchange at women's music festivals, helped with student orientation, or led workshops for a few hundred extra dollars. In my 20s and 30s, teaching what I loved, I was happy. I only felt unhappy when people who earned more for teaching the same course load felt the need to tell me I had failed. At one institution where I taught, a senior faculty colleague wrote a newspaper editorial slamming adjunct faculty as "usually not scholars with an in-depth grasp of the history, ideas, controversies and new discoveries in their discipline that comes with years of research and writing." Sigh!

In that year after Harvard, I was still an active member of the Senior Common Room at Currier House, where I'd been scholar-in-residence for 1990–91. I was also on the faculty at Northeastern, and there my colleagues included Debra Kaufman, Winnie Breines, Laura Frader, and ex–presidential candidate Mike Dukakis. After Harvard dinners at Currier House, I went out to hear talks by Alice Walker, Randy Shilts, Angela Davis, Dr. Ruth Westheimer, the Guerrilla Girls, Erica Jong. Then back to my one room in Somerville, where the upstairs tenants fought and screamed obscenities and blew hash smoke down through my heating vent. At one point, my knapsack was stolen from that house, containing six years' worth of research, my Harvard access card, my last paycheck, and my Minolta camera—although, miraculously, a neighbor later found my research notes discarded in the garbage underneath her house. The contrast between where I worked and how I lived stopped being funny, even though it made a great scene later in my one-woman play. My savings dwindled to the point that I started to count and roll pennies. Ice cream was a luxury; a quarter, found on the sidewalk, meant I could get a doughnut.

Auditioning for academic positions in the middle of nowhere, hoping to win over stern-faced deans so that I could get out of part-timer poverty and into medical benefits, I slowly released my tentacles from their brief suction-cup attachment to Ivy League life, until Harvard's spectacular comforts were but a distant memory. One luxury remained: I kept the black leather easy chair from my year as a Harvard scholar. I am writing in it now.

Revenge of the Women's Studies Professor
a one-woman play by Dr. Bonnie Morris
Saturday, March 9, 1996 • 7:30pm
Bismarck Hotel Lincoln Room
sponsored by GLSTN Chicago

A benefit for Crazy Ladies Bookstore
Dr. Bonnie Morris in:
REVENGE of the Women's Studies Professor
7:30 p.m. Tuesday, November 14
Northern Kentucky Universtiy--University Center Theatre
$3.00
Sponsored by NKU Women's Studies Program

Tickets to *Revenge of the Women's Studies Professor*

8.

Scene Eight, 1993
Teaching Where Hell Freezes Over

After all that, I finally won a two-year job. At a tiny, tiny, wee town in the coldest part of the United States, far from everyone and everything. Now I had a salary again, but nowhere to spend it, because there were no bookstores, coffeehouses, or delis in town. I was the only one of everything I was: the only feminist, lesbian, Jew. Indeed, I was an exciting multicultural experience for the entire campus community, and folks felt liberal simply because they knew me. But I was snowed in all year with no friends and no escape. The highlight of my week was a good speed-skating workout at the ice hockey arena, followed by a hot apple turnover from the Amish farm family whose buggy floated ghost-like down my street.

There was nothing to do, so I attended every single visiting lecture presentation on campus. I went to talks on plant life, ancient skulls, the vanishing cheetah; anything to stay abreast of intellectual life. One bitter winter night I plowed through the snow in my subzero padded jacket to attend something vaguely advertised as a "human rights" talk. And I was astonished to see that the entire hall was packed. Clearly, many professors had required their students to attend. Curious, I unzipped my snow suit and took a seat.

The speakers turned out to be two gay rights activists who were touring college campuses as advocates of gay marriage; they were committed long-term partners, and their arrival on campus had been carefully kept secret. But as I listened to their excellent presentation, I began to sweat with excitement: This would be the perfect moment for me to come out to the entire university!

Sure! Nearly everyone was there—students, faculty, staff. While a few students knew I was gay, I could make a far better statement by supporting our guest speakers with my own public "outing." What better time than this? Everyone in the room was trying their damnedest to look tolerant! It was a brilliant opportunity—no one would beat me up at a lecture on compassion and acceptance! I was going to do it!

I pumped more blood through my pounding heart in the next ten minutes than I had during the entire previous decade, waiting for the inevitable question-and-answer period to begin. Quickly, I raised my hand. "Hi, I'm Dr. Morris, and I appreciated your remarks on the importance of positive gay role models. And because I like to think I'm a positive role model myself, I'd like to take this opportunity to come out as a lesbian professor in our university community." Thus unburdened, I sat back down.

And suddenly, everyone else stood up.

I'll never forget the feeling in my body as, to my utter surprise, this previously apathetic audience rose and gave me a standing ovation.

But I don't know if the lump in my throat came from hearing the applause of my own students—or seeing four lesbians from the next town rush to the exit, car keys in hand, lest I try to make friends with them. They were terrified of being "outed" by an activist like me. They had kids and custody to worry about. They couldn't be my friends.

I was making good money again, but that's what life was like teaching up there.

For two years I taught at this isolated, private university with openly hostile attitudes toward women and women's studies. During the first week of classes, a male student told me to my face that "gays aren't human." Days later, he was expelled for assaulting a female classmate. It turned out to be a typical week there.

I understood, soon after I arrived, that the administration was fully aware of deep-seated misogyny on campus; hiring me was supposed to help solve the problem. (Look! We have a women's history professor now!) It was a lonely, challenging assignment, and I wrote a great deal in my journal about being on display as the token feminist scholar in an otherwise traditional, male history department. Nonetheless, I was grateful to have a job. And I was on a mission, as always, to put a friendly face on women's history. My classes soon filled to overflowing.

Countless students sought me out with personal stories of sexual harassment or belittlement by other faculty and classmates. This made me privy to a range of grievances and Title IX violations that should have been pursued through legal channels; but almost no students were willing to come forward formally. They feared, as so often happens, that their grades or reputations would suffer if they dared to confront a tenured professor about his attitudes toward women. Instead, they quietly changed classes or majors after encountering a professor who openly mocked women in academia. Some just wanted to graduate and get out; I recall with sadness the brilliant senior who had to give an in-class presentation for her final grade in a tough foreign affairs course. She was the only female student, and after she presented her paper the instructor's evaluation was, "None of us heard a word you said; we were too busy looking at your legs."

Quite a few female students also complained to me that they did not have the support of other young women on campus; no one wanted to be labeled a feminist, and any attempts at organizing an undergraduate women's group met with derisive remarks and graffiti about the organizers' sexuality. One popular sorority gave notice that any student enrolled in my women's history classes had to keep their textbooks out of the front parlor so that boys who came calling wouldn't get "the wrong message" about the sorority. My students in this house were hiding in the bathroom, their books for class covered in plain brown wrappers, reading about how women won the right to vote seventy-three years earlier. Scholar Bernice Sandler, who coined the term *the chilly climate for women,* would have found rich material in the environment of University X.

What does, in fact, constitute a chilly climate? First of all, there was the graffiti: in library books, on dining hall desks, on walls. I discovered that a textbook I'd put on reserve in the campus library, Sheila Ruth's *Issues in Feminism,* had these sarcastic words (I've kept the original spelling) scrawled on the title page: *Tell me a fucking Dike that Dieing for some cock didn't write this.* And on the foreword page: *All woman should be either 1)Barefoot and Pregnat or 2) on the street corner sucking and fucking.* If one had the heart to read further, the next page featured a graphic sketch of two men sodomizing a naked woman as they yanked her along the ground on a dog leash. Too late, I realized that every student who had gone to the library and read the assigned chapters in this book had been forced to look at these angry words and images drawn on the title page. And none of them had wanted to tell me about it.

Ordering a bowl of chicken soup on campus was no panacea for my dismay: A serving tray in the dining hall had these words scratched into it with a knife: "Feminism is for ugly dykes." Everywhere, walls and halls reflected these sentiments.

The most frequent complaint I heard from students was that male faculty, including administrators, established this degrading tone with negative comments about women, whether in classes or at high-level meetings where student representatives were present.

My professor was talking about Navajo ways and said he wanted to focus on men: "unlike Paula Gunn Allen who just focuses on women." He had a large smirk on his face as he poked fun at this Native woman poet. How can women be valued if teachers do not value them?

I am the only female in my geology class, and the professor is both anti-feminist and completely biased against girls. He is a firm believer that females cannot succeed in science. I have consistently received the lowest grades in the class, although I am doing the same quality of work as my male classmates.

A student asked me what women's studies classes are like. Before I could respond, two guys answered for me: "They are a bunch of bitter girls who sit around for hours just male-bashing!" I asked if either of them had ever taken a women's history course. "Well, of course not!" they responded.

I am on the campus Judiciary Board, which consists of five males and two females. A student who knew I am a women's studies minor refused to have his case heard unless I stepped down, saying that I would not give a male a fair hearing. I refused to step down, and the dean had to decide the case.

Last year I was the student representative on the Dean Search committee. Two men on the committee said it would be a waste of time to interview any of the qualified women in the candidate pool, that we couldn't possibly have both the college president and the new dean be women. "Our students wouldn't like two feminists in power," they said.

I took a Reasoning class in my junior year and the professor asked us to discuss the date rape poster with the slogan

"No means no." He told us that sometimes No means Yes, and that if a woman is wearing a sexy red dress, how is a man supposed to believe that No means No? I have never taken another course with this man. I changed my major.

I had dinner at a professor's house; other faculty were there, and somehow we got on the subject of the gang rape that took place at a local restaurant. A professor I had known for a week said that men can't really help themselves once they get to a "certain point," and that judges should keep that in mind and not punish rapists too harshly.

I went to high school nearby and ran into my old history teacher today at the basketball game. He had constantly made passes at me when I was a senior, but I proudly told him I was now majoring in history. He asked what I was taking and I told him about my U.S. women's history class. He then laughed, made a sour face, and said, "Why are you wasting your time on a class like that?"

I was in the computer lab printing my term paper for our women's history class. The computer science consultant, instead of helping me, laughed outright: "Why would anyone write a paper on something like that?"

Some students, fed up with these attitudes and concerned that image-conscious sororities dominated campus life for women, created an alternative residence hall called the Women's Center. They were aware that they would encounter mocking stereotypes, and proposed holding an open house for all students to drop by, meet the residents, and discuss issues affecting women at the university. A flurry of incidents followed:

I overheard a group of men discussing the Women's Center open house: "I wouldn't step foot in that house with all those women-lovers." "I'm not going to drink tea with a bunch of male-bashers." "They'll stand by the door with butcher knives and castrate us."

Last night at 4 AM a man broke into the Women's Center house, screamed "Heya, pussies!" and threw ripped-up pictures of lesbian pornography all over our front entry hall. When I reported this in the

office where I am a work-study student, the secretary said, "Well,
but you don't have any . . . gay women living with you, do you?"

We had a message on our answering machine from a
young man assigned to write an article about the Women's
Center house. He said, "If you don't call me back soon,
I'm going to whip it out and shake it at you."

I was wearing a Women's Center t-shirt the other day and a
freshman asked me if I lived there. I responded, "No," and he
said, "Good thing!" His comment shocked me because he's brand
new to college—stereotypes obviously spread quickly. Other
comments I've heard are "I hate those feminist tree-huggers"
and "They're more of a man than we are." My roommates
went over to see what rooms were available for next year,
hoping to get the beautiful third-floor quad. But someone had
written "Dyke Floor" on the wall. And my roommate changed
her mind, worrying about what her guy friends might say.

Young women who chose the more conventional residence of a sorority house still had to deal with cruel remarks and speculation about their
sexuality:

A certain sorority has had to give up their charter and their
house, and there have been outlandish rumors circulating.
"The house could no longer handle their weight." "They
were just too ugly to have composite pictures taken." "The
fat dykes can't recruit any more dykes around here."

Athletics might have been a resource for female empowerment on this
campus, but here, too, the negative attitude prevailed. Many, many students
complained that the women's lacrosse team had to hold a bake sale to pay for
their 1,000-mile bus ride to a tournament, while the men's team flew to the
same tournament, fully funded. The men's athletic fields were quickly plowed
after fresh snowfall; the women were handed shovels and instructed to clear
their own field right before a match. I showed my support for women's athletics by attending every one of my students' games; but when a male colleague

spotted me heading out to an important women's basketball playoff, he commented, "I guess you've got nothing better to do on a Friday night?"

Where to begin? How do we expect female students to excel in an atmosphere of perpetual intimidation and derision? One professor alone cannot cure this illness. And yet I knew my presence made a difference.

What fascinated me was the absolute obsession with lesbianism on campus: Both male and female students were extremely homophobic, convinced that any interest in women's issues—political, economic, social—was proof of homosexuality and should be nipped in the bud. Name-calling was rampant. And yet, as the scene from my play makes clear, there were almost no lesbians in this isolated community.

Just as contemporary Poland has seen an increase in anti-Semitism despite the postwar dearth of a Jewish community—and, in Japan, anti-Semitic publications flourish in the absence of a Jewish population—it is common for lesbian-hating to dominate an environment with no lesbians. Such was the case at University X. There was no visible lesbian subculture, only the very private lives of perhaps two lesbian professors, counting myself, and two gay men on the faculty. But as my students' comments indicated, fighting off lesbian stereotypes took up a ridiculous percentage of their social time. It effectively served to discourage female students from the merest of feminist interests.

Feminism is the bridge which takes a previously non-labeled woman into the realm of name-calling. At this predominantly white, Christian campus, with a socioeconomically homogenous enrollment, lesbian-baiting was almost the only cultural form of harassment students risked. And lesbian identity could be merely implied—an accusation without proof—as distinct from racism. Any woman may be called a lesbian. It is a reputation waiting to happen.

Students' insistence that every resident of the campus Women's Center had to be gay was, then, wildly inaccurate. But as long as the label *lesbian* was understood to be the worst accusation of all, young women hastened to demonstrate behaviors which placed them above suspicion—and this went far beyond having a boyfriend handy. It meant refusing to get involved in activities with other women (aside from sorority life), or in activities that placed women's political interests at the center. It meant an active female participation in name-calling of other women—and vocal dismissal of women's studies as a viable academic major. The pressure to prove one's heteronormativity by producing a boyfriend at any cost also led some young women to make bad choices. Date rape was one unplanned outcome of salvaging a "dyke" reputation. Far more students were rape victims than lesbians, but that was an unpleasant reality no one wanted to believe; instead, most of my male students thought women had an easy ride in life.

> A girl and I were watching an HBO special on date rape. I asked her if she'd ever heard of date rape occurring on our campus because I never hear about it. She said she knew about plenty of incidents, but they were never reported because the victim was so embarrassed. It's hard for me to believe that it actually happens on this campus.

> Getting into bars is easily a woman's biggest advantage. Bouncers let girls in with fake IDs but guys get turned away. And there have been numerous times when I have been driving with women friends who were let off with warnings or a slap on the wrist after being stopped for speeding. And I heard a girl in my government class say that her paper was not going to be done on time but that she could go to the professor and cry in his office. "It always works," she told me. Women use their advantage to get out of trouble.

I had to get out of there. I had to get out of there. But to what?—back to part-time, underpaid adjunct work? That terrified me. And it wouldn't resolve the problems for the ones I left behind, the bright students being cheated of a full college education by faculty who belittled women.

I did two things while finishing out my contract in the snow. I began to write the one-woman play exploring these linked concerns. And I accepted an invitation to spend one hundred days away, on a ship, teaching women's studies for the famous Semester at Sea program. In the coming year and beyond, I would take my curriculum around the world.

9.

Scene Nine, 1993
Women's Studies Goes Global

Look, I came on this voyage to learn about culture, not about women.
　　　　　　　　　　　　　　　—Semester at Sea student, fall 1993

By 1993 I had started to tour with *Revenge of the Women's Studies Professor,* driving to conferences and college campuses around the United States in my faithful Toyota. By then, the poor car was held together with bumper stickers and bungee cords. I'd arrive in some remote university town, perhaps have dinner with other women's studies faculty, and then do my show—sometimes as part of a Women's History Month program, sometimes as a fundraiser for a battered women's shelter or feminist bookstore. The next day I might teach a guest class, answering questions about the issues raised in my play. I seldom earned more than an honorarium of $75 or $100 and a free meal, and I made up the difference in my accumulating travel expenses by selling autographed copies of my script for a few dollars. If the only space students could reserve for me to speak on campus was an after-hours classroom, it was usually still strewn with used soda cans and coffee cups that no one had bothered to clean up. I therefore not only did my own driving, performing, and publicity, but also took a broom and trash pail and swept whatever venue was arranged for me. I would go on to present *Revenge* for the next fifteen years.

But of all the places I performed my one-woman show, the high seas of the Atlantic Ocean off the west coast of Africa presented the most unique challenge. My chair tilted from left to right as waves literally lifted me out

OPPOSITE PAGE: Semester at Sea lifeboat drill, near Japan, 2004 of my seat, giving some scenes unintended emphasis. By the time I finished, I had traveled many nautical miles toward America without ever leaving a small circle of light in the middle of a ship's ballroom. It was December 1993, and I was a women's studies professor on Semester at Sea, finishing up one hundred days aboard the *S.S. Universe* with 480 students and faculty on a global voyage around the world.

What was it like to teach women's studies at sea? To introduce American students to questions of global feminism, enhanced by actual tours through thirteen countries? What happens when a journey around the world awakens deep-seated shame about the female body in otherwise "liberated" students? All of this and more awaited me when I became a visiting professor for the University of Pittsburgh's famous Semester at Sea program in 1993. (I returned to the program again in 2004, taking students to a different itinerary of countries; more on Cuba and Zanzibar later.) When I first sailed with SAS, I was not only highly visible as *the* shipboard feminist but, at 32, I was the youngest member of the teaching faculty—and the only out gay adult. I was a lightning rod for all the tension, debate, and pain surrounding issues we faced in every country—and in our own tight community aboard ship.

Officially, my job, like that of all SAS faculty, was to teach three globally focused courses in my area of specialization and to give a few lectures in the giant daily morning class everyone attended. I taught Women in Society, Sex Roles in International Politics, and a course on ethnic and gender identity in immigration and refugee history. In each country on our itinerary (Japan, China, Taiwan, Malaysia, India, Egypt, Turkey, Russia, Greece, and Morocco), I was responsible for developing field trips related to my courses or serving as guide/chaperone on other faculty trips. This itinerary would take my students into girls' schools, battered women's shelters, and women's bookstores; into the private homes of local feminist writers; and through the complex labyrinth of sex-segregated custom in five Muslim lands. I was ecstatic.

I did not have to seek out the SAS students who were already involved academically in women's studies. These students found me. My cabin was open to their frequent visits and my company solicited at mealtimes. In my classes, the discourse on gender politics was exciting, challenging, fresh. In each port, our explorations of gendered space included adaptations and compromises few male students had to negotiate: Should we wear headscarves? Insist upon entering cafés in communities where "nice" women did not usually dine out? Too often, my students and I endured indescribable sexual harassment and mockery of Western women. But since this first journey was well before the events of September 11, 2001, we saw our challenges and anxieties as opportunities to interrogate sex role customs; concerns about terrorism were less pressing, less of a boundary line.

Barely a week into the voyage, my function as a women's studies professor began eliciting the same old backlash. Fall 1993 students reeled from my opening lecture in the Global Studies course we all attended daily: I had simply repeated statistics from a UN report: "Women constitute half the world's population, perform nearly two-thirds of its work hours, receive one-tenth of the world's income, and own less than one–one hundredth of the world's property."[1] I also reported that in countries such as China and India, where population control of one-billion-plus is a constant concern, the preference for sons over daughters had created dramatic problems of sex-selective abortion and female infant neglect—skewing national gender ratios and (in China) filling orphanages with unwanted girls. I reminded the shipboard community that most peoples believed in some version of a male God and a divinely ordained hierarchy of sex roles, so that women's efforts toward modernization and change could be opposed as blasphemy. These were global family issues we'd encounter in every port, but in 1993, many students were shocked to hear such subject matter introduced.

One irate young man approached me afterwards and complained, "Look, I came on this voyage to learn about culture, not about *women,*" as though the two were mutually exclusive. From then on I had a reputation as a "male basher," and when I was called on to add perspectives on women (during lectures where no information on local women was otherwise included), students rolled their eyes. Some who were not enrolled in my other classes felt angry at having women's studies forced upon them. Until we actually arrived in our

---

1. The actual quote from paragraph 16 of Document 70 is:

> The effects of these long-term cumulative processes of discrimination have been accentuated by underdevelopment and are strikingly apparent in the present world profile of women: while they represent 50 per cent of the world adult population and one third of the official labour force, they perform nearly two thirds of all working hours, receive only one tenth of the world income and own less than 1 per cent of world property.

From "Report of the World Conference of the United Nations Decade for Women: Equality, Development and Peace, held in Copenhagen from 14 to 30 July 1980." In *The United Nations and the Advancement of Women, 1945–1995* (New York, N.Y.: Department of Public Information, United Nations, 1995), 243.

first ports—we had an initial fourteen-day Pacific passage from Vancouver to Japan—students felt entitled to inform me that I was exaggerating, inventing, or otherwise manipulating facts and figures to serve a negative agenda. I was fascinated to observe that while students disinterested in courses such as music, anthropology, or economics agreed that those fields made important contributions to understanding our world, studying women—half the world's population—commanded little respect. Even by 1993, plenty of students hailed from North American colleges where women's studies programs didn't exist; some had never had a woman professor. They were convinced I was not a scholar with useful information to share, but a member of the political lunatic fringe poised to humiliate them with canards about male power.

Almost every male student who initiated a conversation with me made fun of my stance as a feminist; one told me point-blank, "Did anyone ever tell you that you look just like Hillary Clinton?" Another said he had registered for my advanced sex roles class "in order to make sure that a balanced viewpoint is included." This actually came across as a better motive than that of the student who comfortably informed me that he had no interest in women's history at all, but needed some "easy" distributive credits at a class time that allowed him to sleep in after partying all night. Students stuffed my shipboard mailbox with clippings on women's issues, as though only the resident authority should read such articles; but I was the Keeper of All Things Female by then. Wearily heading up to bed one night during that first week, I overheard four students arguing about the politics of leaving a communal toilet seat up or down. When someone suggested, "Look, let's go get Dr. Morris and have her decide," I fled to the sanctuary of my cabin.

Nine days into the voyage, I noted in my journal:

It's barely ten AM and I've already refereed six gender confrontations. One student informed me that Rush Limbaugh was a god, and that this voyage would be a wake-up call to "the girls" that they had it good in America and should just shut up. Another student told me that when he married he'd expect his wife to bring him a beer every night, and yet another said he'd forbid his future wife from working. One student dared me to name any influential women in U.S. history other than Abigail Adams. Another announced that he had every intention of visiting brothels in Asia, showing off a fat wallet of dollars set aside for this purpose. And to round

off the morning, a residence hall counselor found this item in
the Suggestion Box: "Can we have a Statutory Rape Night?"

All in the first hour of my workday, halfway between
Alaska and Japan.

Male students' fraternity t-shirts from home colleges were an ongoing
free speech problem. Often printed with graphic alcoholic and sexual messages, these items were not only worn in every public space aboard ship (classrooms, labs, the dining halls) but also into every country we visited, even
when diplomacy or sheer common sense suggested leaving inflammatory
slogans on board. Aside from the usual graphic depictions of throwing up,
urinating, and one spectacular rendition of all the *Peanuts* characters drunk
from a keg debauch and groping each other, t-shirts I saw every day included:
"If you're not wasted, the day is." "A day without a buzz is a day that never
was." "Greeks do it with their brothers and sisters." "Pearl Harbor Day: Let's
get bombed!"—actually worn into Japan by one student. "No fat chicks." "Ten
reasons why beer is better than women." And a women's symbol covered with
a circle-and-slash—no women allowed here.

But there was a learning curve on the ship—and this proved true on both
of the voyages I joined. After visiting the third or fourth country, witnessing
brutal conditions of poverty and women's double burden of childbearing and
manual labor, most students saw that I wasn't making up statistics on global womanhood. And those who were already women's studies majors were
awakening to a different kind of backlash: the sexual taunting they received
when, as unveiled Western women, they left the ship unaccompanied by male
guardians. Their experiences in traditionally Islamic villages of India, Egypt,
Turkey, and Morocco led to some of our most important class discussions.

As an American woman, I am automatically a sex object.
I am walking pornography! I always loved, even craved,
being different and standing out in a crowd with my green
eyes and red hair. Now I know how it feels to be viewed
as different because of my ethnicity, my nationality.

Every man stared at me and commented on my
appearance. In one sense, I was very flattered, but in
another I was upset. They made me feel dirty.

This is the first time I can remember wanting
to feel ignored; to be inconspicuous.

I don't believe that women should have to cover up simply
because men can't control themselves, but I also decided
to wear a headscarf along with my jeans and boots. I
received numberless marriage proposals and come-ons.

When I did have the chance for conversations with people,
I jumped right into intellectual material. It was fascinating
to watch a man go from talking to me as my gender, to
marveling at the fact that I am an educated woman, and then
eventually to engaging me in real political conversation.

Of course, sexism also exists in North America. Rather than blaming street harassment on men's national identity or religion, my students looked critically at what Hollywood films taught such men to believe about American women, particularly if they had only been exposed to film classics like *Pretty Woman, Indecent Proposal, Striptease,* and *Debbie Does Dallas* (not to mention the deadly, sexually insatiable anti-heroines of *Basic Instinct* and *Fatal Attraction*).

The lines I received from men were outrageous, sometimes funny
or absurd, but always with the undercurrent of sex, sex, sex. I was
not prepared for the onslaught of suggestions and gestures. Movies,
television, and of course pornography make it appear that we
American girls are empty-headed sex maniacs with plenty of money
and libido. So I can't condemn men who are acting according to
what they think they know about me; I condemn my own society for
exporting a degraded image of American women on a global scale.

I consider myself rather hip and laid back, and honestly
thought I could handle the verbal harassment in the bazaars.
And I did. But when one man put his palm on my butt
and buried his mouth in my hair, I lost it. I'm mad at that
man, but I'm also mad at the fact that our American media
may have helped him feel entitled to do what he did.

We are conditioned to believe we are helpless and endangered.
I traveled through Marrakesh with three girls who were afraid of
every man and screamed when touched accidentally by the hood
of a coat. This is not being a cautious traveler, or having normal
concerns as an American woman exploring an Islamic country—it's
a victim mentality which allows us to be exploited as tourists.

For all their immersion in global studies, many Semester at Sea students came aboard as very inexperienced travelers. Having paid their tuition, they did not expect any gendered limitations on their personal freedoms while exploring the world through a college program. Most painful were class discussions about actual or attempted assault: the price paid for a friendly smile or for walking into the wrong café.

It was an absolute nightmare, being stalked, and the
scariest part was that we were really yelling and hitting—
and no one stepped in to ask if we needed help.

It took so much energy to survive the tour. Men yelled
things at us like "Fuck you," "Fuck your country," and
even "Fuck your haircut!" My heart was racing. And I
was pissed because they knew they could scare me.

In the marketplace, we found that simply saying "No" and
walking purposefully away did not deter men. They grabbed
our arms and blocked our paths. It was more physical and
personal than the harassment we encountered in some countries;
one young man screamed, "Fuck you and your mother, you
American woman!" All day, his words rang in my ears.

I thought if I got into a troubling situation all I had to do was find a
woman to help me. But my first impression was the absolute lack of
women in public. There were no women in sight. A man grabbed me
and demanded that I enter his shop. When I pulled back he snarled,
"Whore," and then more people began to swear at me: "Your fathers
are bastards, you're all filthy whores." There was nowhere to turn.

Male students, too, recounted tense moments of seeing their female class-mates reduced to sex objects or being jeered as Americans themselves. Some men were relentlessly offered sexual services, or invited into bars that turned out to be brothels.

> You know, the women from the ship were advised to travel with male companions, but nobody considered the safety of those male escorts! I was actually scared. It was stressful the whole time, and that is an understatement. Many shop owners harassed me because I was traveling with several American women, some of whom were of Asian heritage; I was asked if I'd be willing to sell my wives or give up one of "my" Asian women since I obviously "had so many." Some spice dealers offered me special mixtures meant for orgies; seeing me with more than one female companion, some shopkeepers grabbed their balls and made up songs praising my sexual stamina! I dealt with the stress by making jokes. But I was terrified—even ashamed.

On the ship, in class, students began to express new appreciation for certain freedoms they enjoyed in the United States—the ability to go out in a sleeveless top without being called a prostitute, for instance. Predictably, we moved into debates about the veil and the burqa: As Western women, did we associate genuine liberation with more revealing styles of dress? For all their insistence on the right to show their flesh, many of my students were at war with their own bodies. How many of these "liberated" young women berated themselves, daily, for being fat? One particular class trip led to new perspectives.

In two different countries, Turkey and South Korea, I took my students to a women's bathhouse—traditional sites for steaming, soaking, singing, and exchanging gossip in a safe, all-female atmosphere. We stripped down, wrapped ourselves in small white towels, and entered a dream interior of marbled domes and slabs. Spigots gushed hot water into ancient pools, sloshing over our bare skin. Considering how difficult it was to meet local women or to find activities free from intrusive male comments, I thought these bathhouse outings would be regarded as highlights of the voyage. I was wrong. The vulnerability of physical nakedness after days of verbal assault brought up every student's anxiety about her perceived imperfections. Although they were accustomed to co-ed freedoms back in the United States—even demanding them as a natural right—few of my students knew how to relax and network in woman-only space.

In our class discussions after the bathhouse trips, the very students who routinely wore bikinis on the ship's pool deck (or insisted upon the right to wear tank tops into Cairo) confessed their horror at having to undress in front of other women. Embarrassment, physical competitiveness, deflated body image, and complex eating disorders made it almost impossible for anyone in my class to admit to liking her own body. How could we expect to start a dialogue with women from different cultures when we often resisted discussing the differences among ourselves?

> I was not at all prepared for the tension and anxiety I found! Each woman had a different reaction to the Turkish bath: some guarding themselves in a fetal position, petrified with modesty, while others tried to escape or hide. We who had been wary about sexual harassment in this country were now wary of each other!

> Competition and obsession with fashion and fitness has made the American woman fear her own body. I'm not sure what kind of statement that makes about sisterhood in the United States!

> Why do we have false modesty in the company of other women? If a woman had showed up in a miniskirt in Puritan days she would have been flogged or called sinful. Yet in our lifetimes, on TV the Brady Bunch daughters wore miniskirts to school and were considered so pure.

But several students were able to connect the events of the day with a powerful awareness of ongoing female culture.

> An image I will never forget is watching a Turkish mother bathing herself and her two young daughters. It was right out of a painting; one of the most beautiful and poignant images of womanhood. At times like this I realize how lucky I am to be a woman. Yet I literally had to force my roommate to go through with this trip to the bathhouse.

> An older lady came playing a tambourine, singing and dancing, and to my shock I found myself dancing around the room

with all the other women. In the course of that hour I had
a cultural experience that transcends being clean. I learned
how women in a male-dominated society still meet and speak
freely. These seemingly "powerless" women developed a
way to unite in a subtle way. I saw a child dance with her
mother, aunt, and grandmother, becoming part of centuries
of women who relax and speak freely in the bathhouse.

Having a forum to address these situations and scenarios reinforced support for gender studies classes—the very curriculum some students loudly
mocked when first aboard.

Women's studies as a field gained converts daily after the third country
we visited, and by the end of the voyage, students I had never interacted with
in a classroom begged to talk with me, to share writings, or to sit in on a few
classes. (I might add that giving certain lectures poolside, in my best theatrical
tones, helped attract interest.) Simply put, students were shocked by the secondary status of most women in the world—women they observed, in every
country, sagging under heavy burdens of wheat, rice stalks, animal fodder,
market vegetables, plus a basket of manure and, always, a hungry babe at the
breast. Meanwhile, men might stop work to smoke and drink in cafés where no
woman was ever permitted to enter, sit down, and relax. Instead, to preserve
female modesty (and since there were no "women's" cafés), a street vendor
with a waterjug on his back and a community cup on his belt poured drinks
for veiled women doing their marketing in Casablanca's ancient streets.

Looking at global studies through the lens of gender is now an accepted
academic component for any student concerned with economic development,
AIDS prevention, and education in debt-burdened countries. But in the early
1990s, most American students had to see the global gender divide with their
own eyes before they admitted there might be a place for women's studies as
an academic specialty.

At least one of my students promised me she would petition for greater
expansion of women's studies courses, both in the Semester at Sea program
and at her home campus:

We have matured. We now realize that the role of women
is an important subject to be researched—before entering
any country. Look how frustrated the non–women's studies

students were when they met gender customs they didn't comprehend. Learning about separate female culture ahead of time helped us behave appropriately, meet other women, even, in some unusual situations, protect ourselves.

As the voyage lurched to an end and students quietly turned inward, studying for final exams, I presented my one-woman play on the dance floor of the ship's ballroom, reminding everyone that a backlash against women existed in America, too—but in recognizable stereotypes we could all confront with humor. Some of my students also spoke, explaining that it was everyone's responsibility to address the harassment of women back home. Would we now be better attuned to domestic sexism?

This led to an interesting response. Some students wanted to write a skit about the sexual catcalls every woman had encountered in port. We ended up with a readers' theatre exercise during our last class, taking turns reciting out loud the worst, most offensive pick-up lines we had endured as female travelers. It was a remarkable ritual, sharing long lists of insults to our bodies, our chastity, our sexuality, our nationality as Americans, permitting us to relax into relieved and incredulous laughter. "Taking back the harassment" served two purposes. It reminded each student that she (or he) had not been alone in attracting unwanted street comments. And our blunt retelling of the most hurtful language took away some of its sting. Recalling both intentional dishonor and desperate sales techniques, we roared over the juxtaposition of "Hello, may I fuck you?" and "I will of course marry you immediately, but first, kindly buy this handsome rug from my shop."

We completed the ritual by sharing useful advice for other women travelers—especially visitors from the West, who might be stepping into more gender-segregated streets for the first time.

Walk like you have a specific mission. But enjoy every minute.

Use good judgment.

Don't be afraid to go out—but take one friend.

Don't overplan. Let it happen. Watch and observe how other women behave.

Don't meet the eyes of men you don't want to talk to.

Don't be too loud or too noticeable.

Be sure to arrange home stays in order to
meet local women and their families.

One thoughtful young woman added, "Send a letter to yourself after you have safely returned from the voyage and have the post office hold it for one year." Several added, "And don't forget to call your mom and thank her for raising you."

As a student, I was traveling free of family or domestic
responsibilities, with time to hang out—in cafés, bars,
and restaurants, which were places belonging more to the
male sphere. I had to keep in mind the unmerciful nature of
women's work, along with the substantial demands women
face of expanding scarce resources to meet family needs.
All of this created obstacles for our contact time with other
women. And it took me several countries to realize this.

Oppression of women is a universal norm. And where there is
a male standard, women become a special interest group.

Every country has policies to protect women's rights. But
they're not enforced because women are not the enforcers!

I traveled with my boyfriend, and often thought I was missing
out on the "true" woman's experience—maybe I should
be traveling alone, or with other females. But then, what is
that unaccompanied female experience? Jeers, harassment,
catcalling. So, traveling with a man actually gave me the perfect
perspective to see how most women live every day of their lives.
They must always deal through a "superior" male, whether
father, husband, brother, or son. Only once in a great while
do the women of the world get a vacation from the men.

In honor of Eve, I handed each woman an apple.
Then we danced.

10.

Scene Ten, 1995
Educating President Clinton

I teach at George Washington University now. We have a nationally ranked women's basketball team, sometimes in the top ten in the country. I attend every game, cheering the players on. Most of them have taken at least one of my classes.

The first year I was at GWU, men's and women's games were scheduled on the same day, back to back. Huge crowds showed up on Homecoming Day. I didn't expect to find a metal detector, and tight security. Had someone phoned in a bomb threat? What was up? A security officer explained: The president was coming. President Clinton had brought Chelsea to a game. After all, the White House is just six blocks from our gym.

The men's game ended in victory for GWU, and there was a long break before the women's game began. To my disgust, as usual, most fans rose to leave now that the men had played. I watched the president walk into the bleachers, shaking hands with nearly everyone. How easy it would be to go up and meet him! And didn't I have something I needed to say?

So, I pushed my way through the crowds, thrust out my hand, and said, "Hi, Mr. President! I'm a women's studies professor here at the university. It would mean so much to us, to our women's team, if you would stay and watch the

Opposite page: Onstage at the National Women's Music Festival, Indiana University, 1993. Photo by Toni Armstrong Jr.

women play. Don't leave now. Show your daughter, and the
world, that you support Title IX and women's sports!"

"Well, I'd like to stay," President Clinton
told me. "But I have this meeting . . ."

I glanced at the clock. Our women were about to take the
court. "That's fine, Mr. President, I understand. But you can watch
the first few minutes of the women's game." I couldn't believe I
was giving a direct order to the president of the United States of
America. But he sat back down! And stayed to see the women win.

Bill Clinton became the first president to call in his
congratulations to the champion women's basketball
team of the NCAA tournament that spring. Yeah, I'd like
to think I had a little something to do with that. That's the
kind of good influence, as a women's studies professor,
that I wanted to have; that I still have, I hope.

Yep. I gave a direct order to a U.S. president. It was one of the most exciting moments in my life. And this scene in the play is the one that audiences,
too, find exciting: You did *what*? You said *what*?

I'm a women's studies professor, but I'm also a citizen. And when the
commander-in-chief plans to walk out on the women's team, I feel entitled to
protest. It says a great deal about the value placed on women when a national leader makes a special trip just to cheer on local male athletes—and then
heads for the exit once the women's game begins. But when a short version
of this encounter was published in Rivka Solomon's popular anthology *That
Takes Ovaries!*, I received angry mail from some readers. "Why didn't the Secret Service prevent you from approaching our president?" "What made you
think you had a right to speak to him that way?"

I can only say that I spoke on behalf of all the female athletes I knew and
worked with—for by 1995, I was teaching a brand new women's studies class
called Athletics and Gender. I've now taught this women's sports history seminar every semester for more than thirteen years. Enrolling in the class are top
female athletes (and many male athletes, too) from every sport at both George
Washington University and Georgetown.

Why develop a curriculum on women's sports? Because, thirty-five years
after Title IX law began the slow process of opening funds and opportunities
for girls and women in athletics, we're still hearing slams against sportswom-
en. As the Don Imus controversy of spring 2007 showed us, female athletes

starring on one of the best college teams in the nation can be dismissed as ugly, their femininity impugned; at worst, reduced to the stereotype of "nappy-headed ho."

Women who arrive at college courtesy of an athletic scholarship encounter challenges male athletes never face—challenges to their sexuality, to their very right to play ball—sometimes every day. Moreover, a women's team can have a terrific record and yet, in the middle of its championship season, play to near-empty bleachers—part of the reason I was adamant that our nation's president stay in his seat for the women's game.

Sports culture, more than almost any other facet of American society, defines (and limits) notions of masculinity and femininity, from recreation to body image to professional opportunity to media coverage of heroes. I wanted to design a class that would engage both male and female students, those who might otherwise never take a women's studies course—football players, for instance. Wrestlers. Athletic trainers. Guys like Carl Elliott and Robert Diggs, GWU's star basketball players, who did enroll. Guys who might one day soon coach women, or raise daughters. It turned out that male students, even more than women, were grateful for a classroom environment that let them talk about the pressures they, too, experienced as campus jocks.

Looking at American history through the lens of sports is one way students may observe systematic exclusion based on gender (and race). Rarely, in the past, were the best female athletes in the country permitted to compete, to get college scholarships, to earn a living at the professional level; nor were their events covered by sports journalists or broadcast on television. This unfinished revolution is still painful to see. To understand how athletic women's experiences are routinely cut out of the story of American sports, just consider the following incident.

A Man's World

In 1997, as female athletes prepared to celebrate the twenty-fifth anniversary of Title IX, African Americans were also commemorating the fifty-year anniversary of Jackie Robinson's integration of major league baseball. Exhibits across Washington, D.C., paid homage to Robinson's legacy and to other black athletes who had dared to cross the color line in pro sports. That spring, ABC's *Nightline* news program hosted a "town meeting" on the topic of racism in American sports history, filmed at historically black Howard University and moderated by Ted Koppel. College athletes from the greater D.C. area were invited to be part of the studio audience, and I attended along with a busload of GWU students from my Athletics and Gender class, plus several players from GWU's top-ranked women's basketball team.

The auditorium was packed with male and female athletes, former athletes, sports fans, students, coaches, and parents, black and white. But onstage, there was not a single woman among the retired coaches and athletes who spoke about racism in sports. Not one woman had been included in that panel of experts, and in the hour that followed, as my students looked to me with questions brimming in their eyes, there was absolutely no mention of the countless black *women* who overcame double discrimination to set world records.

Just when I thought my head would explode from frustration, the audience participation portion began. Up rose the co-captain of the GWU women's basketball team, Tajama Abraham, who politely asked Ted Koppel why black women were not represented on this important occasion. Were they not part of this story? Had they not experienced racism, as black athletes?

The audience roared its approval of these questions. And, caught off guard, Ted Koppel offered a stunning reply: "We can't cover everything in an hour, and let's face it, *sports is a man's world.*"

Here was a white man telling a black woman who led her team to the Elite Eight, twenty-five years after Title IX became law, that her effort and sweat and experience and victory were simply not part of history—or history as it should be told by our national media. Her exclusion from the story was not because she was black—no, that would be wrong. It was because she was female, and let's face it, sports is a man's world.

The audience, genuinely outraged, booed and hissed. The producer—a woman—reddened with embarrassment. The GWU contingent recoiled in horror—*no one* disses Tajama! But I could not have asked for a better illustration of why women's history courses are needed in every school. When one of America's most powerful journalists suggests that only the male experience equals the whole truth, when this choice to render women's lives invisible is broadcast from our nation's capital, the public message we all hear is loud and clear: Women as athletic leaders and heroines do not belong in history—or on TV.

This is how women are written out of the record. That night, we watched it happening, on *Nightline*.

My students rode back to campus that night in a state of shock, which they expressed on the bus in tellingly different ways—loud talk, rigid silence, or angry tears, depending on personality. Days later, when a male sports fan wrote to the *Washington Post* complaining that women's basketball was getting too much coverage, GWU's co-captains materialized in my office doorway and asked for help in drafting a feisty letter to the editor. The *Nightline* experience had turned them into activists. Their dignified letter in defense of women athletes was instantly published, highlighted within a special, bordered box.

When I ask my Athletics and Gender classes what sort of discriminatory attitudes the (women) students encountered growing up as young female athletes, their anecdotes tumble out:

> What amazes me is the argument that girls are kept out of rough sports because they aren't "safe." At my high school, only the boys were allowed on our nice practice field. The award-winning field hockey team had to use an abandoned elementary playground so full of holes and garbage that it did not pass regulations for the season. There were countless injuries from ankles twisted in rabbit holes, and a teenager was found dead in the woods by our "field." I'd hardly call it safe for girls—just definitely second-best.

> As captain of the soccer team here, I have to deal constantly with lesbian stereotypes and homophobia in sports. Sometimes I just get sick of constantly having to prove my heterosexuality. And it makes me realize what some of my teammates who really are lesbians go through every day.

> One of our crew coaches is an Olympian, about 5'8" and 150 pounds of solid muscle. All the rowers respect and idolize her. However, I have been in situations where bony girls look at her muscled quads with horror and disdain, making me want to shout, "She's an Olympian, you idiot."

> There was one girl on our soccer team when we were really young. Her mom wouldn't let her continue playing soccer in high school because then her legs would get too big and she wouldn't be elected homecoming queen. Her mom had gone to our school, you see, and had been homecoming queen back then.

> At my high school I confronted the vice-principal at the boys' soccer game and asked why he always went to watch

the boys but never came to see the girls play. He gave me a week of detention, saying I had embarrassed him in front of parents. But he never came to see a girls' game.

Our coach is vocal about the fact that he only recruits pretty girls. There is no secret about it. There was one incident where a prospective athlete came to visit; she was great athletically, but not beautiful. And after she left our coach made the comment that yeah, she was talented, but he could not look at her face for four long years.

If I arrive at practice in a bad mood, the men say, "You must have PMS." One guy even said that a woman couldn't be president because having PMS, she might jeopardize the security of the United States. This guy trashes his room when he loses a match—is he somehow more stable and controlled?

On my high school baseball team we had a coach straight out of East Baltimore who made us line up for sprints on Thursdays and then punished the slowest guy by making him run the entire field with a bra on. "Bring out the brassiere!" he'd scream, grabbing his crotch and humiliating unpopular freshmen. He did this when the priests weren't around, but we got the point—the worst thing was to be compared to a girl.

I am on the women's basketball team and work out and lift at Gold's Gym. Yesterday I was on a weight bench doing a chest press with dumbbells, and a man said, "Can you please hurry up? I need that bench to do some serious lifting."

I'm on the women's dance team here, and recently a dancer was caught smoking while in uniform and benched for the next three games. She was scolded by our coach, by the head of the Student Association, and by certain faculty members, all of whom told her that her behavior was shameful and "disrespected the university." Meanwhile, a male athlete sexually assaulted a woman and then played in a major game a few days later.

I was at a collegiate athlete awards dinner for Division I NCAA water polo and a man referred to me as a "plus-size model type." The entire table went silent. I am a size 8.

At age 7, I loved gymnastics, but the rigorous training lasted for eight years. Through a strict diet and strenuous workout routine, my coaches helped me delay puberty and praised me for not menstruating. We were forced onto diets, with abusive weekly weigh-ins. All this was hidden from the gymnasts' parents, but when mine found out what was going on, they forced me to quit. Within a few months I grew an inch, gained ten pounds, and finally got my first period.

I work in a sports bar where I have never once seen one damn women's game on any of the giant-screen TVs.

My speech teacher flat-out told me that I couldn't possibly know enough about football to do play-by-play commentary for my final class presentation.

I had another run-in with a male who thought I was sports-illiterate because I'm a girl. I was wearing a light purple sweater to work and this guy in the elevator said, "Bet you don't even know you're wearing Baltimore's color. Bet you don't follow the Super Bowl." I informed him I was a Ravens fan who had never missed a game.

I took a look at the *Sports Illustrated* website and was very disappointed by the lack of attention to professional women's sports. So I typed in "women" to see if I could find links to additional articles, but what I got was a blank screen and the message "Women is not a valid keyword!" When I typed in "Men," I was sent directly to the NBA site.

It would be easy, in a class like this, to keep the focus contemporary, examining only today's sports controversies—which are many and varied. But Athletics and Gender attracts both women's studies majors (some of whom are new to sports history) and athletes (some of whom are new to women's history). So we begin back in the seventeenth century, when it was a crime in our New England colonies to jump or play on a Sunday. Exercising on the Lord's Day in Vermont, for instance, was punishable with fifty lashes and a fine; the Puritans actually burned James I's Declaration of Sport. How did we become a nation where it's a mark of American manhood to spend Sunday watching violent football?

That first month of basic U.S. history guides the students to a better understanding of the uniquely American sex roles and policies defining sports opportunities. By the mid-nineteenth century, with science edging out religion as the determinant of proper female behavior, medical authorities were banning sports for women based on their belief that overexertion threatened the delicate feminine reproductive system. Heavy physical activity might damage the womb. But this protective attitude never applied to slave women, to factory girls, to working children, to exhausted farmwives, or to any of the other American females who were intimately acquainted with physical overwork (and abuse). Specific ideals set up for middle-class white women governed the evolution of sports culture; thus, the official policy for athletically gifted girls became *exercise in moderation.* In short, girls' rules.

Nice girls weren't supposed to sweat, spit, swear, roughhouse, compete to win, expose bare legs or arms, break records set by males, tour professionally, or follow a career that put childbearing on hold even temporarily. Fitness was synonymous with beauty, and a bit of wholesome contact sport such as field hockey might be permissible at elite girls' boarding schools, but the Olympics? Distance running? Full-court basketball? Athletic scholarships to college? Forget about it. Moreover, the design of women's clothes guaranteed discomfort, immobility, and nagging dictates of modesty. And beauty standards changed every few years, particularly as Hollywood film culture emerged and the celebrity movie star became someone to imitate.

In the second month of class we turn to the complex definitions of masculinity and femininity in American society today. If athletic prowess signifies manhood, are women, as the "opposite" sex, required to be smaller and weaker? Does female achievement threaten men? Mariah Burton Nelson took on that question with her groundbreaking text *The Stronger Women Get, the More Men Love Football.* Do men resent female intrusion into the locker-room realm? Can one succeed as an athlete yet fail as a woman?

I've lost count of how many female athletes say in class, "My mother is proud of me and brags about my athletic trophies, but she also begs me to stop weight training so my arms will fit into the little frilly blouses she wants me to wear." The obsession with femininity guarantees that a female athlete isn't treated the same way a male sports hero might be evaluated. Media, family, friends—everyone scrutinizes a powerful woman; she's cast as unnatural. And women's achievements in strength and physical power are being regarded with new suspicion, now that star athletes like Marion Jones have been charged with the use of performance-enhancing drugs.

But while girls still get pushed to choose ballet, gymnastics, figure skating, tennis, field hockey, and so on, more and more are also making news as basketball and soccer players. That's awakened parents to the possibility of sports talent paying their daughters' way through college. And it's turned entire families into advocates for greater female opportunity in sports—a wave of "sports feminism" that's been cresting ever since the early 1970s, which saw the passage of Title IX law and Billie Jean King's victory over Bobby Riggs.

Title IX is the main focus of my sports class in the last month of the semester. This key amendment to the Education Acts of 1972 has mandated equal opportunity for more than thirty-five years, and yet confusion over its meaning pits male wrestlers against female softball champs in an ongoing gender-equity debate about money. Simply put, Title IX forbids any educational institution receiving federal funds from discriminating on the basis of sex. Originally, the law was not intended as a solution to wild disparities in athletic opportunity (the standard statistic from the Women's Sports Foundation is that pre–Title IX, 99% of all athletic budgets went to boys' sports, leaving 1% for girls). Instead, Title IX meant to address discrimination in admissions and academic programs—such as publicly funded law schools, medical schools, and math/science magnet schools that refused to admit qualified women. It never occurred to most Americans, in 1972, that by 2009 women would outnumber men at most universities, so Title IX's early legal interpreters suggested that sports programs should offer "proportionate" funding: If women were 30 percent of a university's students, they merited 30 percent of the athletic budget. The possibility of setting aside one-third of the sports jackpot seemed less dramatic, more feasible, than an even split of absolute equality. Plus, there were two other prongs for Title IX compliance: Schools could demonstrate a gradual history of adding women's sports, or prove that they had willingly satisfied the demands/interests of female athletes at their campus.

At George Washington University, we go by the gradual-history-of-adding-sports prong; but adding women's teams over time has been facilitated by GWU's purchase of a satellite campus, Mount Vernon, which has field space for women's softball and soccer and lacrosse. GWU is also unique in having no men's football program: We are very much a basketball school, with outstanding female and male teams. But at schools where football eats up the majority of a total athletic budget, there's no room to add additional teams or build additional fields and, where women have suddenly begun to outnumber men on campus, the numbers game gets rough. Sports administrators sometimes make the decision, then, to abandon less popular men's sports (diving, gymnastics, wrestling) in order to reserve some funding for women—a choice which doesn't really increase women's team opportunities, but very definitely decreases men's. It's this elimination of existing programs which has led to deep resentments and understandable cries of reverse discrimination.

Ironically, most female athletes in my classes today aren't aware of Title IX. The majority flunk my "What is Title IX?" quiz on day one. They are living beneficiaries of a statute they haven't paid attention to, taking for granted that *of course* women can go to college, play sports, win scholarships, major in engineering, apply to law school. Today, both male and female students see test scores and family income, rather than gender, as the only barriers to university admission. However, male students now bring horror stories to class about friends at other universities whose teams were cut "due to Title IX." These male athletes experience women's gains as their own losses. And they have support from many conservative groups, some of which have issued a call for revisiting Title IX law. Critics of any reduced funding for male athletes insist that men care more about sports, and are hurt more when they're denied the opportunity to play.

Under the administration of George W. Bush, Secretary of Education Rod Paige supported changing the rules of Title IX compliance to include school surveys as a measure of whether female students even want to play sports. Unfortunately, these surveys are sent by e-mail, so a student who deletes what looks like "spam" will have her lack of response registered as lack of athletic interest. In this way, and by surveying women only, a university might claim that sports equity is uncalled-for—that sports is, after all, meant to remain a man's world.

In a society increasingly competitive over allocation of benefits (and judgmental toward anything smacking of affirmative action), male athletic opportunity is a right—and female athletic opportunity a "special right." Or, as Donna Lopiano, the then executive director of the Women's Sports Foundation, told *Time* magazine in 2003, "It was O.K. for women to have equal opportunity only after every boy who wants to has the right to play and never loses that right."[1]

Title IX has definitely increased the presence of women in law school; although most of my students arrive in class unfamiliar with Title IX, a good number of them choose law school as their next step after earning a women's studies degree. Caryn McTighe Musil, senior vice president at the Association of American Colleges and Universities, marked the 35th anniversary of both

---

1. Michelle Orecklin, "Now She's Got Game," *Time* (Mar. 3, 2003): 58.

Title IX and *Ms.* magazine with an essay titled "Scaling the Ivory Towers," noting that "in 1970, women earned only 14 percent of doctoral degrees, but today earn nearly half. . . . In medical schools the numbers jumped from less than 10 percent to nearly 50 percent, and law school numbers from about 7 percent to nearly 49 percent."[2] For students who are part of that law school surge, submitting a Title IX term paper on sex discrimination and sports has made all the difference in making their application materials stand out.

Last week, I attended a congressional hearing on the future of Title IX. The first thing that struck me was the small size of the room and the enormous number of people who had come to watch. It was symbolic of Title IX itself—lots of women, lots of interest, lack of accommodation! So there I was, a Georgetown athlete, and I had to sit on the floor!

As a male athlete, I still believe that Title IX was crafted by liberal women's groups that forced women into male-dominated arenas simply for the sake of equality. It's a quota system attempting to force females into things they may not be interested in.

I am a biology student and can state that from my perspective, women were never expected to be science majors at Georgetown. There were never any women's bathrooms built into the classroom building where I am required to do my lab work, and a broom closet had to be converted for us.

I was a high school junior the first time I heard of Title IX, and I graduated in 2000, not 1975! But the law is now tinted green—both with competition for scholarship money, and with the envy of male athletes.

Women are not aware of their rights under the law! I wasn't aware of Title IX until I went through the NCAA clearinghouse for college. The court my volleyball team shared with the basketball boys was swept for their practices every day, but we had to beg for a broom to sweep our courts ourselves before championship games. And I had no idea that I might be able to do something about this.

---

2. Caryn McTighe Musil, "Scaling the Ivory Towers," *Ms.* (Fall 2007): 44.

Today, I regularly watch my student athletes play. It's both moving and painful to see the women transcend obvious differences in facilities, funding, and fan support to win regional and national acclaim. At GWU, men and women play in the same athletic center—packed to the rafters for men's games, far emptier when women (now ranked in the top sixteen, nationally) take the court. Across town at Georgetown, it's an uglier disparity. Men play in the fabulous Verizon Center downtown, a venue served by the Metro subway and offering regular seating, food concessions, and media broadcasting. The women play in old McDonough Gym, served by no Metro stop and with limited guest parking. At one recent game I attended, the ancient tape of the national anthem broke. There was no backup tape, singer, or pep band; indeed, no cheerleaders—they were all over at the Verizon Center with the men's team. There were uncomfortable plastic bleachers, and the tiny snack stand ran out of pizza. During an important game against nationally ranked Connecticut, the game had to be halted when the scoreboard malfunctioned. In such ways, an Ivy League school makes its priorities clear.

Discussing women's history with Fidel
Castro, 2004. Photo by Tony Fiorini.

Conclusion
Mainstreaming Women's Studies in America

There is a dangerous myth going around this country that sexism doesn't exist anymore, that we have gotten past it and that "alarmist" feminists are an outdated nuisance. Warnings like "Oh, watch out—here comes the feminazi!" abound in our culture, as if for a woman, entitling yourself to an opinion puts you on a par with followers of the Third Reich.

—Margaret Cho

We are, indeed, a frightwig of a movement. And I fear that educated women will continue to be too dangerous.

—Catherine Stimpson

For fifteen years, I've toured with my script—using up my frequent flyer miles and a couple of great blazers, but never losing my enthusiasm for this project. From city to city, campus to campus, and country to country, I've talked and then listened, learning that the backlash against women's studies is similar for students and faculty no matter where their classroom is on planet Earth. Female students the world over often experience a threefold backlash—against the burgeoning ratio of women in higher education, against women's studies as their choice of academic specialty, and against educated women's successful entry into professional fields once entirely controlled by men (sports, politics, law, business, the sciences, military leadership, diplomacy, engineering, architecture, and religious vocations).

One should not stereotype women's studies, or feminist theatre, for that matter, as a means for airing grievances. The idea behind presenting *Revenge of the Women's Studies Professor,* after all, was to celebrate teaching women's history, against all odds, and despite situations of hostile or hilarious bias. But for most audiences, there's a thin line between documenting backlash and celebrating success. The group relief in having an opportunity to share those feelings, those common campus experiences, spills out—sometimes lasting for days of networking wherever I've been a guest speaker. At the University of Kentucky, for example, where I tried out some additional stage scenes in fall 1995, I noted in my journal afterwards:

> Heads nodded again and again. I heard responsive gasps and chuckles of recognition. If only someone had videotaped the brainstorming that followed! Graduate students and faculty alike led a spirited discussion that lasted for hours. One woman suggested that every campus have an "anecdote scrapbook" so that a national depository of backlash incidents could be compiled! I felt so wired afterwards that I drove home in a sort of hypnotic beeline. En route, I saw a rather stunning shooting star.

In both New Zealand and Iceland, top women government officials came to my show, and arranged for me to be interviewed on national radio; in Israel my dinner companions included Orna Ostfeld, head coach of the Israeli women's basketball team, and Tal Jarus, a noted activist in Israel's gay rights movement. International audiences, while offering boundless hospitality and patiently listening to English-language presentations, do appreciate a visitor's effort to speak the local lingo. That meant opening my show with bumbling but sincere speeches in Icelandic or Hebrew or Maori or Gaelic, or, here at Gallaudet University in D.C., in American Sign Language.

The questions fired at me post-performance were always startling. Some women's studies advocates in Ireland were excited to talk with the first *Jewish* feminist they'd ever met personally, and they wanted to know whether in America it was safe for one to be "out" as a Jew. Icelandic women wanted to know what I thought of their production of Eve Ensler's *Vagina Monologues* (which had been translated into Icelandic as *Piku Sogur* after prolonged debate over the designation *piku* for *vagina*). At Waikato University in New Zealand, the discussion focused on how women's studies programs too often fail to include perspectives from Native American/Maori/Aboriginal Australian women's communities. And at a fundraiser for a battered women's shelter in

Canada, I watched as my hosts distributed pamphlets on sexual violence in a dozen different languages, a reminder that what united women from every ethnic and racial background in that city was the pervasive threat of assault.

After every show, I tried to stay awake long enough to record impressions in my ever-present journal. From my notes on the show at Victoria University in Wellington, New Zealand, 1998:

> Here I am in Paekakariki, North Island, not terribly far from the South Pole, and like all intrepid travelers I've had some challenges to overcome: My luggage never arrived. And where it is now, no one can say. Gale force winds and record floods and rains greeted my arrival in New Zealand, and my only clothes (the ones I was wearing) were instantly soaked. Prue Hyman, my host, gave me a hot bath, a cup of "gumboot tea," and a space heater; it appears that I'll have to do the performance while wearing one of her old kimono jackets!
>
> . . . The play went really well, with a great turnout, including the Chancellor of the University, the head of the city theatre company, and the author Alison Laurie, all in an elegant, teal-blue gallery. The social mingling, afterwards, was charged with drama: All of these women are big fish in the feminist community's small pond. Several women offered to take me out, and the cafés featured snacks I'd never heard of: Milo, hokey pokey ice cream, wedges, takeaway sandies, Magnum Ego bars, feijoa smoothies, lamb burgers, kumara.
>
> On the day I left New Zealand, after a week of performances, interviews, volcano hikes, and tea with a member of Parliament— all in borrowed clothes or my one pair of jeans—my lost luggage finally arrived.

From Israel, a performance at my alma mater, Tel Aviv University, in 1999:

> Wow. Last night exceeded my wildest hopes. I spent the afternoon with a dozen law students in the Gilman cafeteria, telling stories in broken Hebrew; these women have translated women-and-law books from English to Hebrew by hand, a sort of renegade

rabbinical society of scholars bent over sacred (feminist) texts. At show time, I saw that an absolutely packed auditorium awaited me: not a single empty seat. I counted upwards of two hundred bodies. There were soldiers with guns, too; hopefully, the only time I'll ever perform under armed guard. In the crowd were most of Israel's leading feminist activists, one of whom gave me a very long and, I trust, enthusiastic introduction in rapid Hebrew. The play was a smash; everyone laughed loudly in the right places. It was so hot I soaked through my blazer, guzzling from a bottle of "Ein Gedi" water after each scene, hoping a few modifications of overly American-English idioms made the script more accessible. Most moving: the applause at the end, and the long Q & A during which I described being a young student myself at the university at age 20; I took my final exams in that very auditorium, in 1982! I shook hands and gave out my address, e-mail, book order forms, and photocopied playscripts, to dozens of loving people. We stayed so long that we were eventually thrown out of the auditorium by security guards, and spilled out into the halls, where everyone posed for photos with me and lingered for another hour. I was then taken to dinner at a local café by Rachel Ostrowitz, one of the editors of the feminist magazine *Noga,* and Orna Ostfeld, who gave me a team watch with the emblem of a leaping female athlete. Even through all the excitement, and striving to keep up with a lively discussion of sexual harassment (in Hebrew), I noticed with amusement that the café menu featured a corned beef sandwich called a Biting Tyson. I'll have to tell my Athletics and Gender students.

From my notes on Iceland, May 2001:

I'm treated like a celebrity here in this small nation, scheduled to be interviewed later for Iceland's feminist magazine. I'll certainly freshen up first: I'm coated with frozen mud, having accidentally fallen into a glacier after triumphantly riding a real Icelandic pony. At a café, my waiter introduced himself as having been active in the feminist movement and said his son, aged 26, was also a feminist.

Last night I saw the local production of the *Vagina Monologues,* performed in Icelandic—a derivation of ancient Norse, which of course I don't speak. At the end, the three actresses bowed to each corner of the room and then applauded us in turn. Irgun, my host, who had translated the play, led me backstage so that I could meet the actresses and talk with them about my own play and feminist theatre in general. Two of the actresses have 10-year-old daughters and struggle over whether or not to allow them in to see *Monologues;* much talk about the need for proper sex education before puberty. I was honored to shake their elegant hands. It was still bright and sunny at 10 PM afterwards; I heard the call of the snipe, or "horse cuckoo," and was told that hearing it from the southerly direction in spring is a good omen. Hope so; my show is tomorrow.

. . . The magazine interview, with Thora Thorvaldsdottir, went well: but how embarrassed I felt admitting that my own country lacks free health care, lacks day care, lacks universal maternity leave! Thora said that Iceland's main problems include women earning 30% less than men, and the shocking discovery of sex trafficking (women smuggled in from Latvia), which has created new concerns about the sexualization of society. She wrote her own thesis on Iceland's "beauty myth." I was able to meet the entire board of *VERA* (the magazine's title means "to belong"), and they presented me with a CD of Icelandic women's rock bands! There is an actual Women's Building here, a gender equality commission, a gay union, a feminist political party, and so on. I went to the local bookstore for copies of the *Vagina Monologues* in Icelandic, and found that even the salesclerks already knew about me and planned to come to my show; they listened to my radio interview on the national broadcasting station. The "star treatment" is delightful.

Later: The show was overwhelming!! All of the founding faculty of women's studies in Iceland were there, plus students, the women who translated feminist texts into Icelandic, one of Iceland's first female ministers, and the former mayor of Reykjavik, Ingibjorgu Solrunu Gisladottur. She had been an editor of *VERA* as well as part of the Women's Alliance political party. I was privileged to perform in Iceland's own "little theatre," and my tentative introduction in Icelandic ["Thank you for coming, beautiful women"] won loud approval and applause. Afterwards, one historian approached me and said, "Women must tell our stories!" over and over. When I went home at 12:30 that night it was, of course, still light. There was bright blue sky overhead. I finally saw, at age 40, the famous midnight sun.

Having become a sort of international advocate for the women's studies profession, I craved even more opportunities for cross-cultural exchange. And so I went around the world again, accepting a second invitation to teach women's studies with Semester at Sea. To my delight, the instant I stepped aboard for the spring 2004 voyage, I found a markedly different atmosphere from the suspicion toward women's studies I'd felt in 1993. There was no question that gender issues belonged in a global curriculum, and the plight of women living with HIV/AIDS, particularly in Africa, dominated class discussion. Morning lectures typically addressed women in education, economic support for women in developing nations, the cultural valuing of sons over daughters, and religious-based violence against educated women.

As we were headed to Hong Kong on this voyage, I assigned readings such as "Feminisms in a Hong Kong Classroom" by Geetanjali Singh Chanda, who wrote of her own education in now-familiar terms: "Women's Studies was a life-changing experience for me. Other women have also acknowledged that Women's Studies was the most significant of all their academic experiences in changing the way they thought about life. Yet in Hong Kong, there is a continued resistance, not only to the discipline. . . . The student's perceptions of a feminist as 'man-hating,' 'confrontational,' 'outspoken,' etc., are often associated with Western, if not specifically American, modes of behavior."[1] Looking at anti-Americanism in the various cultures we were about to visit, it was easy to see how women's studies might be resisted as a Western innovation to a nation's curriculum. How did that compare, historically, with how women's studies had been opposed in the United States? In our own country, critics had resisted day care, maternity leave, and equal wages for women as Eastern threats: Women's rights meant Communism. What a fascinating contrast!

Over 70 percent of the students aboard ship were female, for that 2004 voyage, and I was not the only professor teaching a women's studies course or examining gender and diplomacy. Still, there was one colleague who sniffed, upon being introduced to me at the first faculty dinner, "Women's studies is *not* a field. And it makes me angry!"

---

1. Geetanjali Singh Chanda, "Feminisms in a Hong Kong Classroom," *off our backs* (Nov.–Dec. 2003): 35–36.

But had conditions improved for women in the lands we visited? Our first port of call was Havana, Cuba; a rare opportunity for Americans indeed. As an educational delegation, we had State Department permission to dock in that country. In a surprise twist, all of us were invited to attend a speech by Fidel Castro himself at the University of Havana—a marathon four-hour monologue with, fortunately, English-translation headsets distributed to the Semester at Sea crowd. At the end of the speech, SAS faculty had the opportunity to pose for a group photograph with Castro. Not sure whether to be apprehensive or flattered, we quickly waved for the camera, expecting to be hustled off by security officials immediately afterward.

Instead, Castro invited a dozen of us upstairs for a refreshing rum mojito or two. Or three. I thus spent an unforgettable afternoon debating feminism, in Spanish and English, with a notorious dictator—my head spinning both from the proximity to Castro (and I don't just mean same country or even room; he kept his hand firmly on my bicep) and the free-flowing Cuban alcohol. Question: What if there were more women in each of our governments? In global positions of power? Response from Castro: "Ah! If women ruled the world, there would be no more war. The maternal instinct is strong!" Coming from a controversial leader, we took this declaration as some took their mojitos: with a grain of salt. For, of course, even as he spoke, quite a few women were already in top positions of power, and were active agents in policies of war. "Maternal instinct" had never been the first phrase attached to Madeleine Albright, Condoleeza Rice, or, earlier, to Golda Meir, Indira Gandhi, or Margaret Thatcher. And this is one of the great, unresolved tensions of feminist history: As women advance into positions once reserved only for men, do they bring a different set of values to the diplomatic table? Or, to be electable/appointable, must women be willing to take lives in the interest of national security?

As the voyage continued, we saw that sheer daily survival, rather than feminist debate, mattered most to women (and men) in the shantytowns of Brazil and South Africa—these women, too, had their burden of poverty additionally weighted with sexual violence and AIDS. When our ports of call changed to primarily Muslim lands, we returned to the question of whether women can rule (or introduce reforms) where merely their presence in public is regulated by strict codes of dress and traditional modesty; in Zanzibar, I led my students past storefront madrassas (Islamic religious academies) plastered with posters admonishing women not to go out unveiled. The posters made very clear, with graphic cartoon drawings, the difference between "good" women and "bad." I had put on a headscarf out of respect for local custom, but my women's studies students, who insisted upon wearing inappropriately revealing t-shirts and shorts in the tropical heat, looked exactly like the posters' warning against corrupt, Western fashion. In time, some of these students rethought their public presentation, and boosted the local economy by purchasing some modest cotton robes.

We had talked about similar issues of choice and custom when I taught on the fall 1993 voyage; but by 2004, more students had been exposed to news reports from regions of the world where women might be killed for going out unveiled. The question of choice for such women was qualified by very real death threats for disobeying custom. The Feminist Majority Foundation initiated numerous protest campaigns in the 1990s, drawing attention to Taliban violence against women; but only after September 11, 2001, with the U.S. military entering Afghanistan, did a White House resident (in this case, First Lady Laura Bush) speak out about the longtime oppression of Afghan women. Gender-based discrimination had, at last, become a legitimate focus of U.S. foreign policy—but primarily as a means to demonize Islam. All of these issues informed the curriculum on Semester at Sea.

Here in the United States, too, the subject of women in history has at last gone mainstream, part of what an educated person must know. In 2006, the Advanced Placement (AP) U.S. history exam taken by thousands and thousands of bright high school seniors made nineteenth-century women's history its central Document-Based Question, or DBQ. As a reader for the AP exams, I knew that certain women's history topics had been incorporated before, but always as one choice out of several options, never as the main essay required of all test-takers. Now, AP high school students at every educational institution in the country, from Christian home schools to elite boys' prep academies, had to immerse themselves in the history of American feminism. Wow!

And yet even with this official blessing of the all-powerful Educational Testing Service, adult men's snickers and sneers were heard throughout the austere gym where my colleagues and I graded AP essays on women's history. "Let's not waste time debating the merits of the exam question," our room leader sighed, acknowledging that some test readers resented treating women's achievements as a scholarly subject. I, of course, felt glorious happiness and vindication beyond description as I read no fewer than 1,500 student essays on American women's contributions to this nation. My Orthodox Jewish colleagues might say that the occasion called for a *shehecheyanu,* the blessing of thanks uttered on special or first-time occasions.

It's a mixed blessing. Although women's history is present at the advanced/honors level, that's no guarantee that non-honors students will get an introduction to women's history before college. In fact, treating it as an advanced subject only serves to perpetuate the concept that feminism is an elitist interest, rather than relevant to every human's journey. Fortunately, the Girl Scouts of America are equalizing access to knowledge by offering women's history unit projects and merit badges, even for their younger troop members. I gave a Women's History Month talk to my niece's Girl Scout troop, and another to her fifth-grade class; Cassidy, who lives and skis in a snowcapped Sierra mountain town, wanted to know if discrimination against girls still exists. She was shocked to learn that just recently, and despite ongoing pressure from women athletes around the world, the International Olympic Committee affirmed its refusal to allow women's ski jump events in the Winter Olympic Games.

So, at this point, there's still no guarantee that my first-year college students will have had any exposure to women's history—outside of a senior honors class. When I quiz them at the start of class each fall, their answers are mixed. *Who went to a high school that taught women's history? Who knows when women got the vote? Do we actually have an equal rights amendment? Who can tell me what Title IX is? When were women first allowed to run in the Boston Marathon?* These are variants of the question asked by my own Women and Society professor at American University, the late, great Muriel Cantor, on our first day of class back in 1980: *Name three famous women—but they can't be entertainment celebrities or, like First Ladies, known for being married to famous men.* I got the gold star for naming Jane Goodall.

Better late than never, this new attention to women's history. But while students are finding more course materials that mention women, there's another negative breeze blowing on campus. Female students now outnumber males at many elite colleges, and this represents progress for girls—but according to concerned experts, it's also a sign that boys are in trouble. What some feminists have called "the presence of women in more than token numbers" threatens the status quo.

It's a stark change from the climate, just a dozen years ago, which produced texts like David and Myra Sadker's *Failing at Fairness,* a study suggesting that our school system, whether consciously or unconsciously, defers to boys as classroom leaders. Now, the opposite view is popular: Our school system must be broken because boys are falling behind. In fact, in 2006, a senior at Milton High School in Massachusetts, Doug Anglin, took this viewpoint to court. He "filed a federal civil rights complaint claiming that the school system unfairly rewarded girls for being attentive and hard-working," and said that it was men's nature to rebel against just following orders to get good grades.[2] As female academic success continues, a new cottage industry of literature blames feminism (and, more credibly, the lack of male role models in young boys' lives) for what one *Newsweek* cover called "The Boy Problem" and Christina Hoff Sommers called *The War Against Boys.*

Frank Deford, columnist for *Sports Illustrated,* responded with humor and satire during an interview on National Public Radio in September 2006: "When this freshman class graduates in 2010, the Department of Education estimates that as many as three out of every five diplomas may very well go to women. Now there are a lot of reasons which may account for this, including the dread possibility that the weaker sex, so-called, may be, well, simply smarter than we dim brutes. But I certainly think that at least some of this scholastic imbalance may be accounted for by the fact that from an early age, boys are directed towards sports and rewarded more for their athletic prowess than for their classroom work."

It's now an open secret that colleges attracting more female than male applicants sometimes reject high-achieving women in order to admit enough men; to keep the sex ratio from becoming skewed further.[3] NBC's Brian Williams addressed this topic in an evening news segment called "The Truth about Boys and Girls" the week of January 16, 2008. Men with poor grades or test scores also win college scholarships in ways women never experience: as football players. Despite the gains of Title IX, top football schools maintaining a team roster of nearly a hundred athletes have no sports equivalent for women. Moreover, the ongoing success of those football teams may bring back male alumni fans as generous donors. Today there are still more male than female alumni due to the generations when Ivy League colleges limited women's enrollment.

Sports, of course, puts a school's name on the map; and with the exception of a few universities such as Tennessee, Rutgers, or Connecticut, school spirit revolves around the men's teams. Frank Deford is right that men are sometimes rewarded for sheer physicality—for instance, as football or basketball stars—although the graduation rate of top male athletes lags far behind that

---

2. Liesli Schillinger, "Daddy's Little Worldbeater," *New York Times* (Oct. 8, 2006): 1 (Style section).
3. Josh Gerstein, "Kenyon's Policy Against Women Stirs a Debate," *New York Sun* (Mar. 28, 2006): 1 (National section).

of female college athletes. The practice of recruiting celebrity athletes who are unprepared to compete academically in college is seen as a scandal by some, as a necessary evil by others. During NCAA basketball's March Madness in 2007, the *Washington Post* featured a sidebar showing men's basketball graduation rates for schools in the Sweet 16 grid: It wasn't pretty. At Georgetown, the overall graduation rate is 93 percent; but for male basketball players, the rate is half that. At UCLA, my parents' alma mater, only 38 percent of male basketball players graduate (the overall student graduation rate is 87%). Not surprisingly, the racial disparities evident in these statistics have prompted calls for reform, and William Rhoden's book *Forty Million Dollar Slaves* is a text I now assign to all my Athletics and Gender students. But there are plenty of sports fans who see no problem in lacking a college degree if one is being offered a salary twenty times that of any campus professor, just to do what you love. And of course female athletes have a better graduation rate than their male peers: There are no million-dollar contracts awaiting women who hope to play in the WNBA.

Some experts see a different problem down the road: Will all these well-educated women find husbands after graduation? William Raspberry's *Washington Post* column has explored this concern. In her book *Creating a Life: Professional Women and the Quest for Children,* Sylvia Ann Hewlett asserts that fewer than one-third of black women earning more than $55,000 a year end up marrying—including Condoleeza Rice. And Andrew Hacker, author of *Mismatch: The Growing Gulf Between Women and Men,* contributed an essay called "How the B.A. Gap Widens the Chasm Between Men and Women" for the *Chronicle of Higher Education.* These pieces are predicated on the musty idea that a woman who does not marry is a failure, or has been unable to attract the right man.

But there are multiple other variables in any sampling of unmarried female graduates, including simple disinterest in marriage, lifelong commitment to another woman, or entering college as an adult returning student who has already been married—and divorced. In fact, a number of my adult students over the years have been women who married young, intending to be traditional housewives, and then were abandoned by their husbands; now they needed that degree to re-enter the job market. The emphasis in the "new" research on educated women sounds fairly nineteenth century: It's nice to succeed as a student, but husband-catching is paramount. That's a sentiment reeking of the sexism American women fought hard to overcome: Robin Morgan's famous anthology *Sisterhood Is Powerful* includes this 1968 quote from Grayson Kirk (former president of Columbia University): "It would be preposterously naïve to suggest that a B.A. can be made as attractive to girls as a marriage license."[4]

Is the solution, then, to retard one's educational goals? And is female self-retardation truly what men seek in a mate? It's certainly not a new dating tip: In the mid-1950s, my mother's algebra teacher wrote in her yearbook: "To a girl who's smart enough not to let the boys know it!"—suggesting that female intelligence is, at best, hidden. There's an element of cunning and deception in this masking of abilities, hardly conducive to honest dialogue in modern relationships. But it seems that women's success still threatens men.

During the hype surrounding golfer Annika Sorenstam's entry into the all-male PGA tournament in May 2003, Ted Koppel once again hosted a special *Nightline* feature, entitled "Not One of the Boys." His opening remarks suggested that the problem was not female achievement by itself, but rather male embarrassment at being bested by a woman: "Most of all, this is about the fragile male ego." The program looked beyond sports to the question of women's growing economic power: What happens when women earn more than men, or have more education, or both? Should women and girls hold back, perhaps voluntarily curtail female progress where equal opportunity to compete has shown they can outpace men? World Cup soccer champion Julie Foudy, a guest on the program, did not conceal her disgust with this line of rhetoric. She declared, "The amazing thing to me is that we're even having this discussion—it's sad."

But looking at *how* men and boys are being affected by the redistribution of power, and how they perceive changes in sex roles assigned to them, is an important part of any women's studies/women's history course. Men are in my classroom and are active participants. Charged with questioning traditional male-female binaries—and to encourage the growing number of young men interested in pursuing a women's studies minor—numerous women's studies programs are changing their name to Gender Studies.

This change has aroused acrimonious debate. Some women's studies faculty believe such a change undoes decades of hard work, or is somehow a

---

4. "Know Your Enemy," a collection of quotes selected by Robin Morgan, in *Sisterhood Is Powerful: An Anthology of Writings from the Women's Liberation Movement,* ed. Robin Morgan (New York: Random House, 1970), 37.

response to critics who jeer, "How come there's no *Men's Studies* department?" Others contend it's the job of feminist professors, whether male, female, or transgender, to interrogate all sex roles. And students themselves can be the most progressive on the issue of encouraging men to major in women's history; student columnist Emily Liner, a contributing editor to the Georgetown *Hoya,* titled one 2008 article "Let's Start Putting the 'Men' in Women's Studies," arguing, "I'd have to say it's a very good thing to have men interested in women's studies. . . . After all, isn't that what the Jesuit ideal of education of the whole person is all about?"

In 2005, Georgetown's women's studies program did change its title to Women's and Gender Studies. We agreed that a Jesuit institution should not bury the word *woman* so long as a stained-glass ceiling existed for females in Catholic leadership, denying their aspirations to the priesthood. Although many Jesuit colleges and universities now have outstanding women's studies programs, schools where tradition dictates installing a Jesuit as the college president effectively bars women from reaching the pinnacle of academic authority. We elected to keep *women* first in our focus. As feminist scholar Mary Daly put it: "Sojourner Truth did not say, 'Ain't I a gender?'"

But well before changing to Women's and Gender Studies, the Georgetown faculty studied how other schools and scholars treated this issue. We found it useful to read a range of essays, including Matthew Gallman and Barbara Vann's "Politics and Pedagogy: The Creation of a Gender Studies Minor at a Jesuit College," Shirley Yee's "The 'Women' in Women's Studies," and Wendy Brown's "The Impossibility of Women's Studies." Scholar Leora Auslander suggested that the moniker *Gender Studies* signified that "faculty and students interested primarily in feminism, primarily in the construction of gender difference, and primarily in gay and lesbian studies had been cooperating for a long time."[5] This cooperative ethic has been both necessary and significant at Georgetown; the university is now constructing its first LGBT resource center, though not without controversy. Shirley Yee's point is that "the experiences of women are rarely studied in isolation."[6]

---

5. Leora Auslander, "Do Women's + Feminist + Men's + Lesbian and Gay + Queer Studies = Gender Studies?" *Differences* 9, no. 3 (Oct. 1997): 1–16.
6. Shirley Yee, "The 'Women' in Women's Studies," *Differences* 9, no. 3 (Oct. 1997): 46.

Where Are We Now?

We've come a long way since 1969, when San Diego State University launched the first women's studies program. In 2006, the National Women's Studies Association received a $275,000 Ford Foundation grant to collect statistics on the current state of women's studies in America (interestingly, the U.S. Department of Education does *not* include women's studies programs in its Center for Education Statistics). The NWSA survey shows that in 1977 there were already 276 women's studies programs in the United States, nearly doubling in number to 525 by 1989, and holding steady at 650 in 2007 (the latest statistics available). The census reports an enrollment of 88,967 students in undergraduate women's studies classes during 2007, with 4,382 majors and 10,493 minors, and 2,668 graduate students. (Still teaching four courses on two campuses with a side of AP exams over the summer, I sometimes feel that I have graded every one of these majors' and minors' papers at least once. Indeed, the NWSA study also confirmed that part-time and adjunct faculty like myself still make up the majority of instructors. Interest, research, and publishing have vastly outpaced departmental funding and tenure.)

For a brief overview, the *Ms.* essay "Transform the World: What You Can Do with a Degree in Women's Studies" (Spring 2007) offers a look at the experiences of women's studies graduates. "The fact that women's studies majors and graduates were persistently asked what could be done with their degrees reflected a continuing ignorance about women's studies as an academic discipline," writes Nikki Ayanna Stewart—a Ph.D. candidate in women's studies, herself, at the University of Maryland. When Stewart spoke with author Deborah Siegel about trends in scholarly feminism, Siegel suggested that "this current generation is bridging scholarship, activism, and *media.*"

That identification with media is definitely something I see when I ask my students today if they can name a feminist role model. They put together an eclectic list: Madeleine Albright, Christine Amanpour, Katie Couric, Ellen DeGeneres, Hillary Rodham Clinton, Eve Ensler, the Indigo Girls, Patricia Ireland, Joan of Arc, Rosie O'Donnell, Nancy Pelosi, Condoleeza Rice, Diane Sawyer, Martha Stewart, Mother Teresa, Alice Walker, Barbara Walters, Christine Todd Whitman, Oprah Winfrey, and "the women from *The View.*" Some can only name women in the music industry (Celine Dion, Sarah McLaughlan, Madonna, Alanis Morrisette, Sinead O'Connor), whereas the athletes list sportswomen (Mia Hamm, Picabo Street, Venus and Serena Williams). One punk rocker rattles off members of alternative riot grrrl bands

(Kathleen Hanna, Alison Wolfe). I'm amused when a student names Jane Pratt, publisher of the successful women's magazines *Sassy* and *Jane:* Jane and I went to Carolina Friends School together, back when we were 10 and 11 and selling our own purple-inked mimeographed 'zines for a nickel apiece.

It doesn't matter to my class whether or not Madeleine Albright and Mother Teresa, among others they've listed, have ever supported or advocated feminist politics. All of the women they name are feminist role models in their eyes because they are *successful women,* celebrated by the media, and quite a few are the first women to attain the position of power that has made them so visible. My students interpret a feminist role model as any woman of public power; a high achiever. But although they're aware of the impact of Condoleeza Rice, they're less familiar with previous black female politicians who paved the way, such as Shirley Chisholm, or Barbara Jordan, or political critic Flo Kennedy. Few are aware that our fiftieth state, Hawaii, was once ruled by queens—or, more recently, represented in Congress by Asian American Title IX advocate Patsy Mink. There will always be a need to place women's empowerment in historical context; to relate the stories of countless women who paved the way for others and contributed cherished aspects of our identities as Americans. Is it necessary to know women's history? To understand the lives of the less famous? You bet—especially if you're a girl who thinks that no one like you, somebody female, Asian, black, Latina, gay, ever left that kind of mark on U.S. history before now.

Despite my students' long lists of *who* might be a feminist, when I ask, "What does a feminist look like?" they don't picture Geena Davis. They're quick to reply that a feminist is angry, man-hating; someone confrontational, who genders all issues and demands special privileges. The B words surface: *butch, bitch, bitter.* Because they don't wish to be perceived as any of these things, my students do not call themselves feminists.

Until they leave school.

Entering the Real World of earning, after learning, is the wake-up call that real discrimination still exists. After graduating, my former students write to me in the middle of the night:

> My boyfriend is doing his medical residency, and I often hear comments about female med students from the other residents' wives. These women play a role in keeping other women down! Here's what they have to say about doctors' wives who might want to continue their own education: "They should be

at home to greet their husbands!" "Women going to graduate school are wasting time, especially if they want to have kids." "They are taking a man's place in the program." "Going to law school when you're married, that's just selfish." "Why should I go back to school? My husband will make plenty of money." Professor Morris, how far have we really progressed?

Fast forward through women's history to the twenty-first century. We have Nancy Pelosi as the first woman Speaker of the House, and a former First Lady and now U.S. Senator, Hillary Clinton, ran for president. Yet the "women's magazines" I see are obsessed with how quickly Katie Holmes lost weight after her pregnancy.

Women have always represented a good half of the population. On sheer numbers alone we could have had significant power if we could band together and work as a united group. But we have been divided, focused on fighting against one another instead of making progress for the entire body of women. I will take this issue away and use it in my life after college, remembering that working together with other women is a more "profitable" way to reach my goals.

This morning I was at the Supreme Court listening to oral arguments of a case I'm interested in. It really struck me, as I looked up at the black-robed justices behind the large, omnipotent bench, that I was staring at a bunch of men. With Justice O'Connor gone, gender inequality is much more noticeable. Will the fact that there are more educated women in society carry over into positions of power? As a man, I came into your women's studies class influenced by my mother and older sister, both bright, strong women.

For those still in high school or college, perhaps just beginning to think about taking a women's history class, the same old backlash looms—or I wouldn't be hearing the same old stories from my cross-country audiences. Even at the most egalitarian universities today—those with scholarly support for female students, and a record of hiring and tenuring accomplished female faculty—contempt for high-achieving women is a constant part of life. College women's daily lives are shaped by the communities they inhabit, and backlash occurs in places as unavoidable as public transportation. I'll never forget a long bus ride from an airport to a campus, during which our shuttle driver, noticing my magazine, announced to one and all that "Barbra Streisand is ugly as sin! Put a bag over her head, though, and I'd do her!" Comments like these remind women of all ages that appearance, sex appeal, and male approval are the criteria for acceptance—to hell with talent, effort, and critical artistic achievement.

Even for those who pass the beauty test, rumors still persist that all women's studies students and faculty are lesbians. Let's examine this notion: Only women who date women read books about the history of traditional family arrangements? For most of what's published in the women's history field is about *heterosexuality*: marriage, divorce, pregnancy, birth control, child care, welfare—textbooks with titles and subject matter like Marilyn Yalom's *A History of the Wife*.

And critics who think you just have to be gay to get an easy A in women's studies are dead wrong: Sexual orientation doesn't really help with the last draft of that term paper about national security and female suicide bombers. Studying women's history requires hours of immersion in very unsexy topics: the maternal death rate, slavery, factory strikes, seventeenth-century colonial law. We do talk about smashing the patriarchy, some of the time; but as with all academic endeavors, the first rule of women's studies is that you'll sit quietly and read a lot. Our primary orientation? Being studious.

It can be amusing sport to turn the stereotype on its head. If you must love women to venture into women's studies, then shouldn't classes be packed with straight men, hungry to read about centuries of beautiful womanhood? Or loyal sons, honoring their mothers? Plus, the assumption that all women's studies professors are gay is another old canard. All but one of my graduate school professors were married to men. Even now, I have perhaps two openly gay colleagues out of twenty, a percentage barely in step with the national average. Historian Gerda Lerner once pointed out that "male thinkers are never judged by their lifestyles," and this is worth exploring. Men who teach men the history of other men are engaged in objective scholarship, timeless truths, the Socratic method. Their brotherhood is celebrated in movie after movie: *Dead Poets' Society; Goodbye, Mr. Chips; The Paper Chase*. Yet women teaching women the history of women are subjective ideologues, merely pushing lesbianism. And let's not forget that in America, a scholarly woman who lives in partnership with one woman forever may be socially reviled, whereas a male athletic celebrity who becomes HIV-positive after having hundreds of anonymous female partners may win a prestigious appointment to the Presidential AIDS Commission and appear in glossy magazine ads.

Finally, there's still resistance to introducing women's history as a normal, vital subject critical for understanding a world inhabited by both girls and boys. Elementary and middle school hallways must reach beyond the present tokenism of Women's History Month if we are serious about equal education. Journalist Peggy Orenstein's book *Schoolgirls* examines the dilemma for public school teachers who try to expand classroom resources: "Because I include women, I'm seen as extreme. If I took those lessons out and concentrated only on men's experiences for a whole year, that would be 'normal.'"[7] Elsewhere in her report, Orenstein mentions a teacher who suggests that boys perceive equality as a loss. This was my experience as a young professor, when my student "Ralph" complained that my lectures on women in U.S. history (three classes out of thirty-three) diluted important class time with faddish trivia.

What can you do to improve the climate for women's studies? I'll end with the list of seven questions I always offer for discussion when I travel with my play. Remember, it's never been easier to connect with other like-minded folk, to share solutions: The internet has made it possible for me to chat with women's studies faculty in Mongolia, Malaysia, Cuba, South Africa, Turkey, all while I'm still in my pajamas sipping morning coffee. The State Department regularly calls me to give an educational overview on American feminism to female government activists from Yemen, Zambia, Japan. Through distance learning, Saudi Arabian princesses are writing response papers to my videotaped lecture on female athletes. These links to global activism, to a sisterhood of scholars, are the greatest rewards of earning a women's history degree. As musician Mimi Baczewska reminds us, "It's a very long song that we can sing, to celebrate the women of the world."

1. Is there a women's studies program at your school? If the answer is yes, how are the students and faculty perceived? Would you consider taking a course? What would your expectations be—of the teacher, the readings, your parents' reactions to your studies? If there are no women's history courses on your campus, why not?

2. If you are already in a women's studies course, have you experienced teasing or stereotyping? Do you view those comments/jokes as silly and unimportant, or do they really bother you? How do you represent the women's studies program, if anyone asks? Do you read your course textbooks in a public place?

---

7. Judy Logan, San Francisco's Everett Middle School, quoted in Peggy Orenstein's *Schoolgirls* (New York: Doubleday, 1994), 258.

3. Do you have particular role models, teachers, or friends in your life who identify as feminists? Do they conform to ideas about "feminists" in the media? Why or why not?

4. What messages did you get in your home life about woman's place in society? Growing up, were you encouraged to excel at school? Were you aware that many schools were closed to women and girls until recently? What does a scholarly woman look like?

5. How safe do you feel on campus? What precautions do you take, if any? How do you handle street harassment as you commute, travel to other lands, work and conduct research?

6. What would happen if every woman told her story?

7. Will you tell yours?

Bibliography

Addams, Jane. *Twenty Years at Hull House.* New York: Macmillan, 1910.

Aisenberg, Nadya, and Mona Harrington. *Women of Academe.* Amherst: University of Massachusetts Press, 1988.

Armor, John, and Peter Wright. *Manzanar.* New York: Times Books, 1988.

Auslander, Leora. "Do Women's + Feminist + Men's + Lesbian and Gay + Queer Studies = Gender Studies?" *Differences* 9, no. 3 (Oct. 1997): 1–16.

Baumgardner, Jennifer, and Amy Richards. *Manifesta.* New York: Farrar, Straus and Giroux, 2000.

Beck, Lois, and Nikki Keddie, eds. *Women in the Muslim World.* Cambridge, Mass.: Harvard University Press, 1978.

Berkowitz, Tamar, Jean Mangi, and Jane Williamson, eds. *Who's Who and Where in Women's Studies.* New York: Feminist Press, 1974.

Bernard, Jessie. *Academic Women.* New York: New American Library, 1974.

Beyond Beijing: The International Women's Movement. Produced and directed by Salome Chasnoff. Videocassette. Evanston, Ill.: Distributed by Salome Chasnoff/Beyond Media, 1996.

Bordo, Susan. *Unbearable Weight.* Berkeley: University of California Press, 1987.

The Boston Women's Health Collective. *Our Bodies, Ourselves.* New York: Simon and Schuster, 1973.

Brent, Linda. *Incidents in the Life of a Slave Girl.* Cambridge, Mass.: Harvard University Press, 1987.

Bridenthal, Renate, Susan Mosher Stuard, and Merry E. Wiesner, eds. *Becoming Visible.* New York: Houghton Mifflin, 1998.

Brown, Wendy. "The Impossibility of Women's Studies." *Differences* 9, no. 3 (Oct. 1997): 79.

Brumberg, Joan Jacobs. *The Body Project.* New York: Random House, 1997.

———. *Fasting Girls.* Cambridge, Mass.: Harvard University Press, 1988.

Cadick, Jerry. "On Being a Warrior." *Newsweek* (Apr. 14, 1997): 16.

Cahn, Susan. *Coming on Strong.* Cambridge, Mass.: Harvard University Press, 1994.

Cahn, Susan, and Jean O'Reilly, eds. *Women and Sports in the United States.* Boston: Northeastern University Press, 2007.

Cammermeyer, Margarethe. *Serving in Silence.* New York: Viking, 1994.

Carabillo, Toni, Judith Meuli, and June Bundy Csida. *Feminist Chronicles: 1953–1993.* Los Angeles: Women's Graphics, 1993.

Chamberlain, Mariam K., ed. *Women in Academe: Progress and Prospects.* New York: Russell Sage Foundation, 1988.

Chanda, Geetanjali Singh. "Feminisms in a Hong Kong Classroom." *off our backs* (Nov.–Dec. 2003): 35–36.

Chicago, Judy. *Through the Flower.* Garden City, N.J.: Anchor, 1977.

Christ, Carol. *Laughter of Aphrodite.* San Francisco: HarperSanFrancisco, 1987.

Clark, Alice. *Working Life of Women in the Seventeenth Century.* London: George Routledge and Sons, 1919.

Clarke, Edward H. *Sex in Education.* Boston: J. R. Osgood and Co., 1873.

Clinton, Hillary Rodham. Keynote speech at the Fourth U.N. World Conference on Women. Fall 1995. In audio and text format at http://www.americanrhetoric .com/speeches/hillaryclintonbeijingspeech.htm (accessed June 7, 2008).

Collins, Patricia Hill. *Black Feminist Thought.* New York: Routledge, 1991.

Cook, Blanche Wiesen. *Eleanor Roosevelt.* New York: Penguin, 1992.

Cott, Nancy. *The Bonds of Womanhood.* New Haven, Conn.: Yale University Press, 1977.

———, ed. *No Small Courage.* New York: Oxford University Press, 2000.

Cott, Nancy, and Elizabeth Pleck, eds. *A Heritage of Her Own.* New York: Simon and Schuster, 1979.

Davis, Flora. *Moving the Mountain.* New York: Touchstone, 1991.

Diner, Hasia. *Erin's Daughters in America.* Baltimore, Md.: Johns Hopkins University Press, 1983.

Donovan, Josephine. *Feminist Theory.* New York: Continuum, 1992.

Douglas, Susan. *Where the Girls Are.* New York: Times Books, 1994.

Dubois, Ellen Carol, Gail Paradise Kelly, Elizabeth Lapovsky Kennedy, Carolyn Korsmeyer, and Lillian S. Robinson. *Feminist Scholarship.* Urbana: University of Illinois Press, 1987.

DuPlessis, Rachel, and Ann Snitow, eds. *The Feminist Memoir Project.* New York: Three Rivers, 1998.

Echols, Alice. *Daring to Be Bad.* Minneapolis: University of Minnesota, 1989.

Eggen, Dan. "Permissible Assaults Cited in Graphic Detail." *Washington Post* (Apr. 6, 2008): A03.

Eisenstock, Alan. *The Kindergarten Wars: The Battle to Get into America's Best Private Schools.* New York: Warner Books, 2006.

Eisler, Riane. *The Chalice and the Blade.* New York: Harper and Row, 1987.

Embser-Herbert, Melissa S. "When Women Abuse Power, Too." *Washington Post* (May 16, 2004): B01.

Emmett, Ayala. *Our Sisters' Promised Land.* Ann Arbor: University of Michigan Press, 2003.

Enloe, Cynthia. *Maneuvers.* Berkeley: University of California Press, 2000.

Ensler, Eve. *The Vagina Monologues.* New York: Villard, 1998.

Evans, Richard. *The Feminists.* London: Croom Helm, 1977.

Evans, Sara. *Born for Liberty.* New York: Free Press, 1989.

Faderman, Lillian. *Odd Girls and Twilight Lovers.* New York: Penguin, 1991.

——. *Surpassing the Love of Men.* New York: William Morrow, 1981.

——. *To Believe in Women.* New York: Houghton Mifflin, 1999.

Faludi, Susan. *Backlash.* New York: Crown, 1991.

Fausto-Sterling, Anne. *Myths of Gender.* New York: Basic Books, 1992.

Fessler, Ann. *The Girls Who Went Away.* New York: Penguin, 2006.

Gallman, Matthew, and Barbara Vann. "Politics and Pedagogy: The Creation of a Gender Studies Minor at a Jesuit College." *Transformations* 3, no. 2 (Sept. 1992): 47.

Garber, Linda, ed. *Tilting the Tower.* New York: Routledge, 1994.

Gibbons, Meghan. "On the Home Front." *Washington Post* (Oct. 16, 2005): B03.

Gibson, Clare. *Symbols of the Goddess.* Glasgow: Saraband, 2004.

Giddings, Paula. *When and Where I Enter.* New York: William Morrow, 1984.

Gilman, Charlotte Perkins. *Herland.* New York: Pantheon, 1979.

——. *Women and Work.* New York: Harper, 1966.

Guerrilla Girls. *Bedside Companion to the History of Western Art.* New York: Penguin, 1998.

Hacker, Andrew. "How the B.A. Gap Widens the Chasm Between Men and Women." *Chronicle of Higher Education* 49, no. 41 (June 20, 2003): B10.

——. *Mismatch: The Growing Gulf Between Women and Men.* New York: Scribner, 2003.

Harriman, Helga. *Women in the Western Heritage.* Guilford, Conn.: Dushkin, 1995.

Heilbrun, Carolyn [Amanda Cross, pseud.]. *Death in a Tenured Position.* New York: Dutton, 1981.

Henderson, Kristin. "A Woman's Touch." *Washington Post Magazine* (Feb. 24, 2008): 16.

Heschel, Susannah, ed. *On Being a Jewish Feminist.* New York: Schocken, 1983.

Hewlett, Sylvia Ann. *Creating a Life: Professional Women and the Quest for Children.* New York: Tall Miramax Books, 2002.

Higonnet, Margaret, ed. *Lines of Fire: Women Writers of World War I.* New York: Penguin, 1999.

hooks, bell. *Ain't I a Woman?* Boston: South End, 1981.

——. *Feminist Theory: From Margin to Center.* Boston: South End, 1984.

Horowitz, David. *The Professors: The 101 Most Dangerous Academics in America.* Washington, D.C.: Regnery, 2006.

Howe, Florence. Introduction to *Who's Who and Where in Women's Studies,* ed. Berkowitz, Mangi, and Williamson. New York: Feminist Press, 1974.

——. *The Politics of Women's Studies.* New York: Feminist Press, 2000.

Hull, Anne, and Dana Priest. "A Wife's Battle." *Washington Post* (Oct. 14, 2007): A01.

Hull, Gloria, Patricia Bell Scott, and Barbara Smith. *But Some of Us Are Brave.* New York: Feminist Press, 1982.

Jennings, Kevin. "Lessons from a Witch Hunt of the 1920s." *The Gay and Lesbian Review* 14 (Sept.–Oct. 2007): 5.

Karabel, Jerome. *The Chosen: The Hidden History of Admission and Exclusion at Harvard, Yale, and Princeton.* New York: Houghton Mifflin, 2005.

Keddie, Nikkie. *Women in the Middle East.* Princeton, N.J.: Princeton University Press, 2007.

Kerber, Linda. *Women of the Republic.* New York: W.W. Norton, 1986.

Kerber, Linda, and Jade Sherron De Hart, eds. *Women's America.* New York: Oxford University Press, 2000.

Kessler-Harris, Alice. Introduction to *The Bread Givers* by Anzia Yezierska. New York: Persea Books, 1999.

———. *Out to Work.* New York: Oxford University Press, 1982.

Kraditor, Aileen. *Ideas of the Woman Suffrage Movement.* New York: W.W. Norton, 1981.

Kubler-Ross, Elisabeth. *On Death and Dying.* New York: Macmillan, 1969.

Leach, William. *True Love and Perfect Union.* New York: Basic Books, 1980.

Lerner, Gerda. *The Creation of Feminist Consciousness.* New York: Oxford University Press, 1993.

———. *The Creation of Patriarchy.* New York: Oxford University Press, 1986.

Levine, Madeline. *The Price of Privilege: How Parental Pressure and Material Advantage Are Creating a Generation of Disconnected and Unhappy Kids.* New York: HarperCollins, 2006.

Lord, M. G. *Forever Barbie.* New York: Avon, 1994.

Lundberg, Ferdinand, and Marynia Farnham. *Modern Woman: The Lost Sex.* New York: Harper, 1947.

Malkin, Michelle. "Candidates Ignore 'Security Moms' at Their Peril." *USA Today* (July 20, 2004), http://www.usatoday.com/news/opinion/editorials/2004-07-20-malkin_x.htm (accessed July 7, 2008).

Manegold, Catherine S. *In Glory's Shadow.* New York: Knopf, 2000.

Marx, Karl. *The Grundrisse.* Trans. David McLellan. New York: Harper and Row, 1972.

Matthaei, Julie. *An Economic History of Women in America.* New York: Schocken Books, 1982.

Meyer, Leisa. *Creating G.I. Jane.* New York: Columbia University Press, 1996.

Morgan, Marabel. *The Total Woman.* Old Tappan, N.J.: F. H. Revell, 1973.

Morgan, Robin. "Know Your Enemy." A collection of quotes in Morgan, ed., *Sisterhood Is Powerful.* New York: Random House, 1970.

———, ed. *Sisterhood Is Powerful: An Anthology of Writings from the Women's Liberation Movement.* New York: Random House, 1970.

Morris, Bonnie J. *Eden Built by Eves.* Los Angeles: Alyson, 1999.

———. *The High School Scene in the Fifties.* Westport, Conn.: Greenwood, 1997.

———. *Lubavitcher Women in America.* Albany, N.Y.: SUNY Press, 1998.

Musil, Caryn McTighe. "Scaling the Ivory Towers." *Ms.* (Fall 2007): 44.

Nafisi, Azar. *Reading Lolita in Tehran.* New York: Random House, 2003.

Nelson, Mariah Burton. *The Stronger Women Get, the More Men Love Football.* New York: Harcourt, Brace and Co., 1994.

Oakley, Ann, and Juliet Mitchell. *Who's Afraid of Feminism?* New York: New Press, 1997.

Obata, Chiura. *Topaz Moon.* Berkeley, Calif.: Heyday Books, 2000.

Odem, Mary. *Delinquent Daughters.* Chapel Hill: University of North Carolina Press, 1995.

Okin, Susan Moller. *Women in Western Political Thought.* Princeton, N.J.: Princeton University Press, 1979.

Okubo, Mine. *Citizen 13660.* Seattle: University of Washington Press, 1983.

Orecklin, Michelle. "Now She's Got Game." *Time* (Mar. 3, 2003): 58.

Orenstein, Peggy. *Schoolgirls.* New York: Doubleday, 1994.

Paglia, Camille. *Sexual Personae.* New Haven, Conn.: Yale University Press, 1990.

Patai, Daphne, and Noretta Koertge. *Professing Feminism.* New York: Basic Books, 1994.

Peril, Lynn. *College Girls.* New York: W.W. Norton and Co., 2006.

Pinchbeck, Ivy. *Women Workers and the Industrial Revolution.* New York: A. M. Kelley, 1969.

Plaskow, Judith. *Standing Again at Sinai.* San Francisco: HarperCollins, 1990.

Pomeroy, Sarah. *Goddesses, Whores, Wives and Slaves.* New York: Schocken Books, 1995.

Quart, Alyssa. *Hothouse Kids: The Dilemma of the Gifted Child.* New York: Penguin, 2006.

Reed, Betsy, ed. *Nothing Sacred: Women Respond to Religious Fundamentalism and Terror.* New York: Thunder's Mouth/Nation Books, 2002.

Reynolds, Michael, Shobha Shagle, and Lekha Venkataraman. National Census of Women's and Gender Studies Programs in U.S. Institutions of Higher Education. National Opinion Research Center (NORC), University of Chicago, 2007.

Rhoden, William. *Forty Million Dollar Slaves.* New York: Three Rivers, 2006.

Robbins, Alexandra. *The Overachievers: The Secret Lives of Driven Kids.* New York: Hyperion, 2006.

Rosen, Robyn, ed. *Women's Studies in the Academy: Origins and Impact.* Upper Saddle River, N.J.: Pearson Prentice Hall, 2004.

Rosen, Ruth. *The World Split Open.* New York: Viking, 2000.

Rossi, Alice, ed. *The Feminist Papers.* New York: Columbia University Press, 1973.

Rothman, Sheila. *Woman's Proper Place.* New York: Basic Books, 1978.

Ruth, Sheila. *Issues in Feminism.* New York: Houghton Mifflin, 1980.

Sadker, Myra, and David Sadker. *Failing at Fairness.* New York: Charles Scribner's Sons, 1994.

Salbi, Zainab. *The Other Side of War.* Washington, D.C.: National Geographic, 2006.

Sanday, Peggy Reeves. *Fraternity Gang Rape.* New York: New York University Press, 2007.

Sandman, Peter, ed. *Where the Girls Are.* Princeton, N.J.: Daily Princetonian, 1965.

Satrapi, Marjane. *Persepolis.* New York: Pantheon Books, 2003.

Schlafly, Phyllis. *The Power of the Positive Woman.* New Rochelle, N.Y.: Arlington House, 1977.

Schneir, Miriam, ed. *Feminism in Our Time.* New York: Vintage Books, 1994.

Scholinski, Daphne. *The Last Time I Wore a Dress.* New York: Riverhead Books, 1997.

Simmons, Rachel. *Odd Girl Out.* New York: Harcourt, 2002.

Sklar, Kathryn Kish. *Catharine Beecher: A Study in American Domesticity.* New York: W.W. Norton, 1976.

Slater, Philip. *The Glory of Hera.* Boston: Beacon, 1968.

Smiley, Jane. "Feminism Meets the Free Market." In *The Mommy Wars,* ed. Leslie Steiner. New York: Random House, 2006.

Smith-Rosenberg, Carroll. *Disorderly Conduct.* New York: Oxford University Press, 1986.

Solomon, Rivka. *That Takes Ovaries!* New York: Three Rivers, 2002.

Sommers, Christina Hoff. *The War Against Boys.* New York: Simon and Schuster, 2000.

———. *Who Stole Feminism?* New York: Simon and Schuster, 1994.

Spruill, Julia Cherry. *Women's Life and Work in the Southern Colonies.* New York: W.W. Norton, 1972.

Stetz, Margaret, and Bonnie Oh, eds. *Legacies of the Comfort Women of World War II.* Armonk, N.Y.: M.E. Sharpe, 2001.

Stewart, Nikki Ayanna. "Transform the World: What You Can Do with a Degree in Women's Studies." *Ms.* (Spring 2007): 65–66.

Stibbe, Matthew. *Women in the Third Reich.* New York: Oxford University Press, 2003.

Stoller, Debbie. Editorial. *BUST* (Oct./Nov. 2006): 6.

Stone, Merlin. *When God Was a Woman.* New York: Harcourt Brace Jovanovich, 1976.

Strum, Philippa. *Women in the Barracks: The VMI Case and Equal Rights.* Lawrence: University Press of Kansas, 2002.

Sutherland, Elizabeth, ed. *Letters from Mississippi.* New York: McGraw-Hill, 1965.

Tilly, Louise, and Joan Scott. *Women, Work and Family.* New York: Holt, Rinehart and Winston, 1978.

Tunnell, Michael O., and George W. Chilcoat. *The Children of Topaz.* New York: Holiday House, 1996.

United Nations. "Report of the World Conference of the United Nations Decade for Women: Equality, Development and Peace, held in Copenhagen from 14 to 30 July 1980." In *The United Nations and the Advancement of Women, 1945–1995.* New York, N.Y.: Department of Public Information, United Nations, 1995.

Walker, Keith. *A Piece of My Heart.* New York: Ballantine, 1985.

Webb, James. "Women Can't Fight." *The Washingtonian* (Nov. 1979): 144.

Weitz, Rose, ed. *The Politics of Women's Bodies.* New York: Oxford University Press, 2003.

Wertheimer, Barbara Mayer. *We Were There!* New York: Pantheon, 1977.

White, Deborah Grey. *Ar'n't I a Woman?* New York: W.W. Norton, 1985.

Winkler, Barbara Scott, and Carolyn DiPalma. *Teaching Introduction to Women's Studies*. Westport, Conn.: Bergin and Garvey, 1999.

Wise, Nancy Baker, and Christy Wise. *A Mouthful of Rivets*. San Francisco: Jossey-Bass, 1994.

Woodward, C. Vann, ed. *Mary Chesnut's Civil War*. New Haven, Conn.: Yale University Press, 1981.

Woolf, Virginia. *A Room of One's Own*. London: Harcourt, 1929.

Wright, William. *Harvard's Secret Court: The Savage 1920 Purge of Campus Homosexuals*. New York: St. Martin's, 2005.

Wrigley, E. A. *Population and History*. New York: McGraw-Hill, 1969.

Yalom, Marilyn. *A History of the Wife*. New York: HarperCollins, 2001.

Yee, Shirley. "The 'Women' in Women's Studies." *Differences* 9, no. 3 (Oct. 1997): 46.

Yezierska, Anzia. *The Bread Givers*. New York: Persea Books, 1999.

Zimmerman, Bonnie, and Toni A. H. McNaron, eds. *The New Lesbian Studies*. New York: Feminist Press, 1996.

Index

Bonnie J. Morris hails from Los Angeles, California, Durham, North Carolina, and Washington, D.C. The first student to graduate from American University with a minor in women's studies, she earned her Ph.D. in U.S. women's history from Binghamton University and went on to teach at Harvard Divinity School, George Washington University, and Georgetown University. She has also been a guest lecturer for two Semester at Sea voyages and two Olivia cruises. Dr. Morris is the author of six books, including *Eden Built by Eves* and *Girl Reel,* both of which were finalists for the Lambda Literary Award, and *Lubavitcher Women in America.*